Xavier Méfret

French and English Self-Taught

Vocabulaire français et anglais comprenant les mots les plus usités dans les deux langues. Précédé de leçons élémentaires de prononciation et suivi d'un abrégé de grammaire

Xavier Méfret

French and English Self-Taught
Vocabulaire français et anglais comprenant les mots les plus usités dans les deux langues. Précédé de leçons élémentaires de prononciation et suivi d'un abrégé de grammaire

ISBN/EAN: 9783337276997

Printed in Europe, USA, Canada, Australia, Japan

Cover: Foto ©Paul-Georg Meister /pixelio.de

More available books at **www.hansebooks.com**

FRENCH & ENGLISH SELF-TAUGHT

VOCABULAIRE

FRANÇAIS  ET ANGLAIS

PRÉCÉDÉ DE LEÇONS ÉLÉMENTAIRES DE PRONONCIATION
ET SUIVI D'UN ABRÉGÉ DE GRAMMAIRE.

PAR

Xavier Méfret

CHEF D'INSTITUTION.

Un travail opiniâtre triomphe de tous les obstacles

SAN FRANCISCO

Job Printing Office of "Le Petit Journal", 603 Washington Street

1882.

RULES IN READING

1. Read slow, and with a great deal of attention, as there are several inconveniences attending fast reading; for you will not only be liable to make many mistakes, but perhaps learn to stammer; neither is it possible for you to pronounce at first, what you are reading, so distinctly as you ought.

2. If you are not sure of knowing how to read a word at first sight, do not guess at the pronunciation of it, lest you should contract the bad custom of miscalling words; but spell it within yourself, before you offer to pronounce it with a loud voice.

3. Be very careful in minding your stops, as they are pointed; or else neither you that read, nor those that hearken to you, will be able to make sense of your reading.

4. Never make any stops between your words where there are none introduced; neither utter *hemms*, nor *haas*, still observing to pronounce what you read with ease, and in the same manner as if you were holding a familiar conversation.

The result of these general rules is, that your pronunciation ought to be *natural*, that is to say, without art or affectation; *clear*, that is to say, distinct and intelligible; *smooth*, that is to say, without any constraint or hesitation.

ELEMENTS OF FRENCH GRAMMAR

PRONUNCIATION

FRENCH ALPHABET

1. The French alphabet has twenty-five letters :—
A, B, C, D, E, F, G, H, I, J, K, L, M, N, O, P, Q, R, S, T, U, V, X, Y, Z.
They are named in French: *a, bé, cé, dé, é, èffe, gé, ash, i, ji, ka, elle, emme, enne, o, pé, qu, èrre, esse, té, u, vé, ikce, i grec, zède.*

Grammatical Signs.

There are three accents, the *acute accent* ('), the *grave accent* (`), and the *circumflex accent* (^).

The *acute* is placed over the vowel *e*, and gives it an acute sound, as in *été*, summer.

The *grave*, placed over *e*, gives that vowel a broad or open sound, as in *progrès*, progress.

The *circumflex* is found over certain vowels that are long, as in *grâce*, grace. It indicates also the suppression of a letter, as *s* in *côte*, (old French *coste*), coast.

The grave accent and circumflex are also used to distinguish from one another certain words spelt alike; as,

des, of or from the.	*dès*, as soon.	*cru*, believed.	*crû*, grown.
du, of or from the.	*dû*, due.	*mur*, wall.	*mûr*, ripe.
la, the, her, it.	*là*, there.	*ou*, or.	*où*, where.
sur, upon.	*sûr*, sure.	*a*, has.	*à*, at, to.

2. The *apostrophe* (') indicates the suppression of the final vowel in any one of the following words; LE, *the*; him, *it*; LA, *the, her, it*; JE, *I*; ME, *me*; TE, *thee*; SE, *oneself*; DE, *of, from*; CE, *that*; NE, *not*, and QUE, *that*, when the next word begins with a vowel or an *h* mute, as, *l'âge* for *le âge; l'honneur* for *le honneur; l'aurore* for *la aurore; l'héroïne* for *la héroïne*. The suppression of *i* occurs in *si*, if, only before *il*, he, it; *ils*, they; as, *s'il, s'ils*.

The *cedilla* (¸) is used under the letter *c*, before the vowels *a, o, u*, to show that the *ç* is to be sounded like an *s*; as in *ça*, that; *garçon*, boy; *reçu*, received.

The *diæresis* (¨) denotes that the vowel over which it is placed, is to be pronounced distinctly from the vowel preceding or following it; as, *naïveté, baïonette*.

The hyphen (-) connects together certain words; as, *suis-je?* am I? *c'est-à-dire*, that is to say.

Pronunciation.

Any printed rules for pronunciation can only be an approximate guide, as there are sounds in our language that have no corresponding sound in the other.

We give below, some of the most useful examples.

a sounds like *a in father.*
ai, ei, sound like *ai in bailiff.*
au, eau, sound like *o in port.*
an, am, en, em, are pronounced nearly like *ang in pang.*
ain, ein, in, im, have no corresponding sound in English.
c is sounded like *k.*
c before *e* and *i* sounds like *s in seven.*
ch sounds like *sh in she.*
d, and *t*, as well as *ds* and *ts*, at the end of words, are mute.
e, unaccented, at the end of a word is generally silent, except in words of two letters.

é with the *accent aigu* (acute) sounds like *a in blade*.
è with the *accent grave* sounds like *e in where*.
g sounds like *g in great*.
g before *e* and *i* sounds nearly like *s in illusion*.
gn sounds nearly like *ni in pinion*.
g and *p*, as well as *gs* and *ps*, are mute at the end of words.
h is mute in most words.
i sounds like *e in me*.
ien at the end of words is pronounced nearly like *ee-ang* in English.
il and *ill* sound nearly like *lli in million*.
If *il* or *ill* is preceded by another vowel, the *i* is not pronounced, and the *l* takes the liquid sound.
j sounds like the French *g before e and i*.
o sounds generally like *o in not*.
ou is sounded like *oo in school*.
oi and *ui* have no adequate sound in English.
on, *om*, are prononced nearly like *ong in strong*.
oin has nearly the sound of *oang* in English, pronounced in one syllable.
qu sounds like *k* in English.
s between two vowels sounds like *z in zeal*.
ss sounds like strong *s*.
un. *um*, are sounded nearly like *un in unction*.
v sounds like the English *v*.
x sounds like the English *x in tax*.
x and *s* at the end of words are mute.
z sounds like the English *z in zeal*.
The terminations *er* and *ez* sound like *é*.
In the monosyllables *je, me, te, le, ne, de, ce, que*, as well as in *lorsque, puisque, quoique*, the *e* sounds like *u in but*. In *les, mes, tes, ces*, it sounds like *è*.
In double consonants, only one is pronounced.

Accents or Stress.

The stress on a particular syllable of a word generally takes place in French on the last syllable of a word, or on the penultimate, if the last syllable ends with an *e* unaccented; as *té* in *fierté*, pride; *ro* in *rose;* *va* in *avare*, avaricious; *ri* in *avarice*.
It takes place also on certain syllables, formed of full-sounding or sonorous vowels, which may be the penultimate of dissylables or the antepenultimate of polysyllables; as *fran* in *Français*, *va* in *élévation*.

Union of Words.

For the sake of euphony the final consonant of a word is sounded with the initial vowel of the following word, as in *vos‿amis*, your friends.
This union of words takes place whenever they are so connected with each other that there can be no pause between them; as, *vous‿êtes‿un‿enfant*, you are a child.
T of the conjunction *et*, and, is never sounded.

Division of Words into Syllables.

In French words a consonant between two vowels is always joined to the following vowel or vowels, as in *a-to-me*, atom; *i-gno-rant* (*gn* is here a liquid consonant); *i-nu-ti-le*, useless; *é-toi-le*, star.
When there are several consonants, the first is joined to the preceding vowel; as in *ac-teur*, actor; *al-pha-bet*.
L and *r*, after a consonant, generally belong to the following vowel, as in *ta-bleau*, picture; *pa-trie*, country.

LEÇONS ÉLÉMENTAIRES
DE
PRONONCIATION
SUR LA LANGUE ANGLAISE ENSEIGNÉE AUX FRANCAIS.

ALPHABET ANGLAIS

L'Alphabet anglais se compose de vingt-six lettres.

A, a = eï.	J, j = djé.	S, s = esse.
B, b = bi.	K, k = ké.	T, t = ti.
C, c = ci.	L, l = elle.	U, u = iou.
D, d = di.	M, m = emme.	V, v = vi.
E, e = i.	N, n = enne.	W, w = deubliou.
F, f = eff.	O, o = ô.	X, x = ex.
G, g = dji.	P, p = pi.	Y, y = ouaï.
H, h = aitch.	Q, q = kiou.	Z, z = zed.
I, i = aï.	R, r = ar.	

Les voyelles sont : *a, e, i, o, u*, ainsi que *y* et *w* à la fin d'une syllable. Toutes les autres sont des consonnes.

REMARQUES SUR LE *Th*. — *Th* a le son dur comme dans THICK, *épais ;* et plus souvent le son doux comme dans THE *le, la, les*.

Pour prononcer le *th* doux, dans le mot *the* qui précède, vous portez la langue un peu entre les dents, en essayant de prononcer le *z* français.

Pour prononcer le *th* dur, vous procédez de la même façon, seulement au lieu de prononcer *th* comme si c'était un *z*, vous le prononcez comme si c'était un *s* français, en maintenant, au début, la langue plus fortement entre les dents, de manière à produire une espèce de vague sifflement.

Dans l'article THE, la prononciation de l'E tient de l'*i* français long quand le mot suivant commence par une voyelle et de l'*e* muet quand il commence par une consonne.

OBSERVATION. On ne peut apprendre la prononciation d'une langue qu'en entendant parler cette langue. Des règles nombreuses sur la prononciation anglaise ne font que la rendre plus difficile, et occupent une place qu'on peut mieux employer.

VOCABULAIRE
FRANÇAIS ET ANGLAIS,

COMPRENANT

Les mots les plus en usage dans les deux Langues.

SECTION I.

DU MONDE EN GÉNÉRAL

Of the World in General.

Dieu, m.	God	Avril,	April
le Créateur,	the Creator	Mai,	May
le Rédempteur,	the Redeemer	Juin,	June
le ciel,	the heaven	Juillet,	July
le soleil,	the sun	Août pr. *oo*	August
la lune,	the moon	Septembre,	September
une étoile,	a star	Octobre,	October
les étoiles,	the stars	Novembre,	November
une planète,	a planet	Décembre,	December
les planètes,	the planets	une semaine,	a week
la mer,	the sea	les jours de la	the days
une rivière,	a river	semaine,	of the week
une source,	a spring	Lundi,	Monday
une fontaine.	a fountain	Mardi,	Tuesday
une montagne,	a mountain	Mercredi,	Wednesday
une colline,	a hill	Jeudi,	Thursday
une vallée,	a valley	Vendredi,	Friday
une plaine,	a plain	Samedi,	Saturday
un élément,	an element	Dimanche,	Sunday
les éléments,	the elements	une heure, (*mute*)	an hour
— le feu,	the fire	un moment,	a moment
— l'air,	the air	une saison,	a season
— la terre,	the earth	les quatre ⎫	the four
— l'eau, f.	the water	saisons ⎭	seasons
le temps,	the time	— le printemps,	the spring
le jour,	the day	— l'été, m.	the summer
la nuit,	the night	— l'automne, m.	the autumn
le matin,	the morning	— l'hiver, m.	the winter
l'après-midi, f.	afternoon	le vent,	the wind
le soir,	the evening	les quatre vents,	the four winds
un an or ⎫	a year	— l'Orient, m.	the East
une année ⎭		— l'Occident, m.	the West
une demi-année,	half a year	— le Midi,	the South
un mois,	a month	— le Septentrion,	the North
les mois de	the months of	une nuée *or* nue,	a cloud
l'année,	the year	un brouillard,	a fog
Janvier,	January	un orage,	a storm
Février,	February	un éclair,	lightning
Mars,	March	le tonnerre,	thunder

l'arc-en-ciel,	the rain bow	un Irlandais,	an Irishman
une ondée,	a shower	un Espagnol,	a Spaniard
la pluie,	the rain	un Portugais,	a Portuguese
la grêle,	the hail	un Italien,	an Italian
la neige,	the snow	un Hollandais,	a Dutchman
la glace,	the ice	un Allemand,	a German
le dégel,	the thaw	un Polonais,	a Pole
la rosée,	the dew	un Suédois, (o-a)	a Swede
		un Danois, (o-a)	a Dane

SECT. II.

D'UN PAYS EN GÉNÉRAL.

Of a Country in General.

		une langue,	a language
		l'Hébreu,	the Hebrew
		le Grec,	the Greek
Un empire,	an empire	le Latin,	the Latin
un royaume,	a kingdom	le Français,	the French
une république,	a republic	l'Anglais, m.	the English
l'Europe, f.	Europe	l'Ecossais, m.	the Scotch
l'Asie, f.	Asia	l'Irlandais, m.	the Irish
l'Afrique, f.	Africa	l'Italien, m.	the Italian
l'Amérique, f.	America	l'Espagnol, m.	the Spanish
la France,	France	l'Allemand, m.	the German
l'Angleterre, f.	England	un village,	a village
l'Ecosse, f.	Scotland	une paroisse, (o-a)	a parish
l'Irlande, f.	Ireland	un hameau,	a hamlet
l'Espagne, f.	Spain	une métairie,	a farm
le Portugal,	Portugal	un champ,	a field
l'Italie, f.	Italy	un pré,	a meadow
la Hollande,	Holland	un verger,	an orchard
l'Allemagne, f.	Germany	un jardin,	a garden
la Pologne,	Peland	une maison,	a house
la Suède,	Sweden		
le Danemarck,	Denmark	SECT. III.	
une capitale,	a capital	D'UNE VILLE EN GÉNÉRAL.	
Paris,	Paris	*Of a Town in General.*	
Londres,	London		
Edimbourg,	Edinburg	Une ville,	a town
Dublin,	Dublin	une cité,	a city
Madrid,	Madrid	ville fortifiée,	fortified town
Lisbonne,	Lisbon	gros bourg, m.	market town
Rome,	Rome	port de mer, m.	sea port
Amsterdam,	Amsterdam	une rue,	a street
Vienne,	Vienna	une cour,	a yard
Cracovie,	Cracow	une place,	a square
Stockholm,	Stockholm	le marché,	the market
Copenhague,	Copenhagen	l'hôtel de ville,	the town house
une nation,	a nation	une église,	a church
un Européen,	an European	une hôtellerie,	an inn
un Asiatique,	an Asiatic	une auberge,	an eating house
un Africain,	an African	un cabaret,	a public house
un Américain,	an American	une taverne,	a tavern
un Français,	a Frenchman	un café,	a coffee-house
un Anglais,	an Englishman	la comédie,	the play-house
un Ecossais,	a Scotchman	la prison,	a jail

les portes,	the gates	un écolier,	a scholar
un pont,	a bridge	un comédien,	a stage-player
les faubourgs,	the suburbs	un bourgeois, (o-a)	a citizen
les habitants,	the inhabitants	un artisan,	a tradesman
un art,	an art	un négociant,	a merchant
art libéral,	liberal art	un joaillier,	a jeweller
art mécanique,	mechanic art	un mercier,	a mercer
la théologie,	theology	un marchand drapier,	a woolen-draper
la philosophie,	philosophy	un marchand de toile,	a linen-draper
la médecine,	physic	un marchand de soie,	a silk mercer
la chirurgie,	surgery	un parfumeur,	a perfumer
le droit, (o-a)	law	un confiseur,	a confectioner
la rhétorique,	rhetoric	un épicier,	a grocer
la poésie,	poetry	un orfèvre }	a goldsmith or
l'astronomie, f.	astronomy		silversmith*
l'arithmétique, f.	arithmetic	un chapelier,	a hatter
l'algèbre, m.	algebra	un colporteur,	a peddler
la géométrie,	geometry	un libraire,	a bookseller
la géographie,	geography	un relieur,	a bookbinder
l'architecture, f.	architecture	un barbier,	a barber
la navigation,	navigation	un perruquier,	a wig maker
la musique,	music	un horloger,	a watch maker
la chimie,	chemistry	un boutonnier,	a button maker
la peinture,	painting	un graveur,	an engraver
la sculpture,	carving	un vitrier,	a glazier
l'imprimerie,	printing	un verrier,	a glass maker
la danse,	dancing	un chandelier,	a tallow chandler
l'écriture, f.	writing	un brodeur,	an embroiderer
un théologien,	a theologian	un tapissier,	an upholsterer
un philosophe,	a philosopher	un fripier,	a clothes-broker
un historien,	a historian	un gantier,	a glover
un médecin,	a physician	un coutelier,	a cutler
un chirurgien,	a surgeon	un fourbisseur,	a sword cutler
un apothicaire,	an apothecary	un potier d'étain,	a pewterer
un avocat,	a lawyer	un chaudronnier,	a brazier
un orateur,	an orator	un drouineur,	a tinker
un poëte,	a poet	un forgeron,	a smith
un astronome,	an astronomer	un serrurier,	a blacksmith
un géomètre,	a geometrician	un maréchal,	a farrier
un géographe,	a geographer	un sellier,	a saddler
un architecte,	an architect	un vanier,	a basket maker
un ingénieur,	an engineer	un tailleur,	a tailor
un musicien,	a musician	un cordonnier,	a shoe maker
un chimiste, (shi)	chemist	un savetier,	a cobler
un peintre,	a painter	un tourneur,	a turner
un statuaire,	statuary	un charpentier,	a carpenter
un sculpteur,	a carver	un menuisier,	a joiner
un imprimeur,	a printer	un maçon,	a mason
maître de danse,	dancing-master	un meunier,	a miller
maître de musique,	music-teacher	un boulanger,	a baker
maître d'école,	school-master	un pâtissier,	a pastry cook
un sous-maître,	an useer	un rotisseur,	a cook

un boucher,	a butcher	un auvent,	a pent-house
un poissonnier,	a fish monger	un plancher,	a floor
un brasseur,	a brewer	le plafond,	the ceiling
un aubergiste,	an inn keeper	un abat-jour,	a sky light
un tonnelier,	a cooper	une boutique,	a shop
un messager,	a carrier	un étage,	a story
un courrier,	a messenger	le premier étage,	the first story
un postillon,	a post-boy	un bas étage,	a ground floor
un batelier,	a waterman	le grenier,	the garret
un bahutier,	a trunk maker	le toit, (o-a)	the roof
un bonnetier,	a cap maker	un appartement,	a lodging
un passementier,	a lace maker	l'escalier,	the stairs
un tisserand,	a weaver	une porte,	a door or gate
un teinturier,	a dyer	porte de devant,	fore door
un pelletier,	a skinner	porte de derrière,	back door
un corroyeur,	a currier	le seuil,	the threshold
un tanneur,	a tanner	un guichet,	a wicket
un cordier,	a rope maker	un gond,	a hinge
un épinglier,	a pin maker	un marteau,	a knocker
un fondeur,	a founder	une serrure,	a lock
un foulon,	a fuller	une clé ou clef,	a key
un cocher,	a coachman	un verrou,	a bolt
un porteur de chaise,	a chairman	un loquet,	a latch
un crocheteur,	a street porter	le vestibule,	the hall
un mendiant,	a beggar	le salon,	the parlor
un instrument,	an instrument	une chambre,	a room
un crayon,	a pencil	un cabinet,	a closet
un pinceau,	a brush	une étude,	a study
un outil,	a tool	une salle à manger,	a dining room
un marteau,	a hammer	une bibliothèque,	a library
un maillet,	a mallet	une garde-robe,	a ward robe
des tenailles, f.	pincers	un balcon,	a balcony
un foret,	a gimblet	une fenêtre,	a window
un vilebrequin,	a wimble	les vitres, f.	the glass windows
une lime,	a file	une fenêtre à chassis,	a sash window
une scie,	a saw	les volets, m.	the shutters
une hache,	an axe	la dépense,	the buttery
une cognée,	a hatchet	la sommellerie,	the pantry
un ciseau,	a chisel	la cuisine,	the kitchen
des ciseaux,	scissors	le garde-manger,	the larder
		le lavoir, (o-a)	the scullery
		la lingerie,	the laundry

SECT. IV.

D'UNE MAISON EN GÉNÉRAL.

Of a House in General.

Une maison,	a house	la brasserie,	the brew house
un hôtel,	a nobleman's house	la boulangerie,	the bake house
un appentis,	a shed	le bucher,	the wood house
un bâtiment,	a building	le four,	the oven
la muraille,	the wall	la cave,	the cellar
le fondement,	the foundation	la cour,	the yard
un coin,	a corner	un puits,	a well
		l'écurie, f.	the stable
		les lieux, m. les commodités, f.	the water closet

— 11 —

un jardin,	a garden	un guéridon,	a stand
une remise,	a coach house	un binet,	a save-all
un atelier,	a work shop	un panier,	a basket
un magasin,	a warehouse	une corbeille,	a flat basket
une poutre,	a beam	une cruche,	a pitcher
un soliveau,	a joint	une cuvette,	a cistern
une latte,	a lath	un vaisseau,	a vessel
un ais,	a board	une barrique,	a barrel
une planche,	a shelf	un perçoir, (o-a)	a piercer
la boiserie,	the wainscot	un buffet,	a cupboard
une pierre,	a stone	une armoire,	a clothes press
pierre de taille,	a free-stone	une commode,	a chest of drawers
une brique,	a brick	un tiroir, (o-a)	a drawer
une tuile,	a tile	un coffre,	a trunk
une ardoise, (o-a)	a slate	une boîte,	a box
du mortier,	mortar	une caisse,	a chest
de la chaux,	lime	une valise,	portmanteau
du sable,	sand	un lit,	a bed
les meubles,	the goods	la couche,	the bedstead
la garniture,	the furniture	colonnes de lit, f.	bed posts
la tapisserie,	the tapestry	ciel-de-lit, m.	top of the bed
un tableau,	a picture	le fond-du-lit,	the tester
un miroir, (o-a)	a looking glass	le chevet,	the bolster
une bordure,	a frame	lit-de-plumes,	feather bed
un siége,	a seat	une paillasse,	a straw bed
une chaise,	a chair	un matelas,	a mattress
un fauteuil,	an arm chair	un oreiller,	a pillow
un tabouret,	a stool	les couvertures, f.	bed clothes
un escabeau,	a joint stool	les draps, m.	the sheets
un marchepied,	a foot stool	les rideaux, m.	the curtains
un banc,	a bench	la ruelle du lit,	the bedside
un coussin,	a cushion	la bassinoire;	warming pan
un tapis,	a carpet	lit de parade,	a state bed
une nappe,	a table cloth	lit de repos, -	a couch
une assiette,	a plate	lit de camp,	a field bed
une serviette,	a napkin	un berceau,	a cradle
un couteau,	a knife	une natte,	a mat
une gaîne,	a sheath	des vergettes, }	a brush
une fourchette,	a fork	une brosse, }	
une cuiller ou cuillière,	a spoon	la cheminée,	the chimney
une salière,	a salt cellar	l'âtre, m.	hearth
un plat,	a dish	la grille de fer,	the grate
une écuelle,	a porringe	les chenets,	the andirons
une saucière,	a saucer	le soufflet,	the bellows
un essuie-mains,	a towel	les pincettes,	the tongs
une bouteille,	a bottle	la pelle,	the fire shovel
une carafe,	a decanter	le fourgon,	the poker
un verre,	a glass	le garde-cendres,	the fender
une chandelle,	a candle	un écran,	a small screen
une bougie,	a wax candle	un par avent,	a folding screen
un chandelier,	a candle-stick	le feu,	the fire
les mouchettes, f.	the snuffers	la flamme,	the blaze

une étincelle,	a spark	
du bois, (o-a)	wood	
un fagot,	a faggot	
une bûche,	a billet	
du charbon,	coal	
charbon de terre,	pit-coal	
charbon de bois,	charcoal	
un tison,	a firebrand	
les cendres,	the ashes	
la fumée,	the smoke	
la suie,	the soot	
bôite-à-fusil, f.	tinder box	
la mêche, l'amadou,	tinder	
une allumette,	a match	
une pierre-à-feu,	a flint	
le briquet, } le fusil,	the steel	
un chaudron,	a kettle	
une marmite,	porridge pot	
le couvercle,	the lid	
le manche,	the handle	
l'anse, (d'un pot, &c.)	the ear	
une écumoire,	a skimmer	
une cuiller-à-pot,	a ladle	
un trépied,	a trivet	
un coquemar,	a boiler	
un poêlon,	a skillet	
une poêle,	a frying-pan	
une casserole,	a stew-pan	
une tourtière,	a baking-pan	
un gril,	a gridiron	
une broche,	a spit	
une brochette,	a skewer	
une léchefrite,	a dripping pan	
un tournebroche,	a jack	
un réchaud,	a chafingdish	
un potager, } nn fourneau,	a stove	
un mannequin,	a hamper	
un seau,	a pail	
un balai,	a broom	
un torchon,	a dusting cloth	
un couloir, (o-a)	a cullender	
une passoire, (o-a)	a strainer	
une râpe,	a grater	
un mortier,	a mortar	
un pilon,	a pestle	
un tamis,	a sieve	
un sac,	a bag	
un cuvier, une cuve,	a tub	

SECT. V.
DU GENRE HUMAIN.
Of Mankind.

Un homme,	a man
homme âgé,	man in years
un vieillard,	an old man
une femme,	a woman
femme âgée,	woman in years
une vieille,	an old woman
un enfant,	a child
petit enfant,	a little child
les enfants,	the children
un garçon,	a boy, lad
une fille,	a girl, lass
jeune homme,	young man
jeune fille,	young girl
les jeunes gens,	young people
l'enfance, f.	childhood
la jeunesse,	youth
la virilité,	manhood
la vieillesse,	old age
un maître,	a master
une maîtresse,	a mistress
le mari,	the husband
la femme,	the wife
un tuteur,	a guardian
un or une pupille,	a minor
l'hôte,	the landlord
un valet,	a footman
une servante,	a servant maid
les domestiques,	the servants
le père,	the father
la mère,	the mother
le fils,	the son
la fille,	the daughter
le frère,	the brother
la sœur,	the sister
l'aîné, m. } l'aînée, f.	the eldest
le cadet, } la cadette,	the younger
le grand-père,	grand father
la grand'mère,	grand mother
la petite-fille,	grand daughter
les parents,	the relations
un oncle.	an uncle
une tante,	an aunt
un neveu,	a nephew
une nièce,	a niece
un cousin, } une cousine,	a cousin

— 13 —

le beau-père,	father-in-law	le sein,	the bosom
la belle-mère,	mother-in-law	la poitrine,	the breast
le beau-fils,	son-in-law	l'épaule, f.	the shoulder
la belle-fille,	daughter-in-law	le bras,	the arm
le beau-frère,	brother-in-law	bras droit,	right arm
la belle-sœur,	sister-in-law	bras gauche,	left arm
le parrain,	the god-father	l'aisselle, f.	the armpit
la marraine,	the god-mother	le coude,	the elbow
un filleul,	a god-son	le poignet,	the wrist
une filleule,	a god-daughter	le poing,	the fist
une amie, f. } un ami, m. }	a friend	la main,	the hand
		main-droite,	right hand
un compagnon, m. } une compagne, f. }	a companion	main gauche,	left hand
		le doigt,	the finger
une voisine, f. } un voisin, m. }	a neighbor	petit-doigt,	little finger
		doigt du milieu,	middle finger
		le pouce,	the thumb

SECT. VI.

DES PARTIES DU CORPS, &c.

Of the Parts of the Body, &c.

		une jointure,	a joint
		l'ongle, m.	the nail
Le corps, .	the body	le ventre,	the belly
un membre,	the limb	le nombril,	the navel
la tête,	the head	le dos,	the back
le visage,	the face	l'épine du dos, f.	the back bone
le front,	the forehead	les reins, m.	the loins
les traits, m.	the features	le côté,	the side
l'œil, m.	the eye	une côte,	a rib
les yeux,	the eyes	la ceinture,	the waist
le sourcil,	the eye-brow	la hanche,	the hip
la paupière,	the eye-lid	l'aine, f.	the groin
la prunelle de l'œil,	the eye-ball	la cuisse,	the thigh
le nez,	the nose	le genou,	the knee
les narines, f.	the nostrils	le jarret,	the ham
la joue,	the cheek	la jambe,	the leg
une fossette,	a dimple	le mollet, } le gras, }	the calf of the leg
la lèvre,	the lip	le pied, .	the foot
lèvre de dessus,	upper lip	la cheville, (du pied)	the ankle
lèvre de dessous,	under lip	la plante, (du pied)	the sole
la bouche,	the mouth	le talon,	the heel
une dent,	a tooth	le cou-de-pied,	the instep
les dents,	the teeth	l'orteil, m. .	the great toe
dents œillères,	eye teeth	doigts du pied,	the toes
dents mâchelières,	grinders	la peau,	the skin
la gencive,	the gum	un os,	a bone
la mâchoire, (o·a)	the jaw	la moelle,	the marrow
le palais,	the palate	la chair,	the flesh
le gosier, } la gorge, }	the throat	la graisse,	the fat
		le sang,	the blood
l'oreille,	the ear	une veine,	a vein
la tempe,	the temple	une artère,	an artery
le menton,	the chin	les pores, m.	the pores
le cou *ou* col,	the neck	un nerf,	the sinew

un muscle,	a muscle	une ride,	a wrinkle
le crâne,	the scull	un bouton,	a pimple
le cerveau,	the brain	une loupe,	a wen
les entrailles, f.	the entrails	une bosse,	a hunch
l'estomac, m.	the stomach	une entorse,	a sprain
les boyaux, m.	the bowels	une égratignure,	a scratch
le cœur,	the heart		
les poumons, m.	the lungs		

SECT. VII.

DES HABILLEMENTS ET DES CHOSES QU'ON PORTE SUR SOI.

Of the Apparel and Things which are worn.

le foie,	the liver		
les rognons, m.	the kidneys		
la rate.	the spleen		
le fiel,	the gall		
la vessie,	the bladder		
les cheveux, m.	the hair		
chevelure, la.	head of hair	Habit complet,	a suit of clothes
la barbe,	the beard	habit de deuil,	mourning clothes
une larme,	a tear	un habit de drap,	a cloth coat
la salive,	the spittle	un habit uni,	a plain coat
l'haleine, f.	the breath	habit galonné,	a laced coat
la voix,	the voice	une veste,	a waistcoat
la parole,	the speech	veste de soie,	silk waistcoat
un gémissement,	a groan	veste de satin,	satin waistcoat
un soupir,	a sigh	un gilet,	a waistcoat
l'éternuement, m.	sneezing	la culotte de velours,	velvet breeches
le hoquet,	the hiccough	culotte de peau,	leather breeches
le sommeil,	sleep	un caleçon,	drawers
le ronflement,	snoring	un surtout,	a surtout
la beauté,	beauty	une redingote,	a great coat
la laideur,	ugliness	un manteau,	a cloak
l'embonpoint, m.	plumpness	la doublure,	the lining
la maigreur,	leanness	les boutons, m.	the buttons
la santé,	health	boutonnières, f.	button holes
la taille,	the shape	une chemise,	a shirt or shift
l'air, m.	the looks	chemise blanche,	clean shirt
la démarche,	the gait	chemise sale,	dirty shirt
le port,	the carriage	chemise garnie,	ruffled shirt
le geste,	the action	le collet,	the neck (of a shirt)
une grimace,	grimace	poignets, m.	the wristbands
les cinq sens, m.	the five senses	manchettes, f.	the ruffles
— la vue,	the sight	le jabot,	the bosom
— l'ouïe, m.	the hearing	une cravate,	a neckcloth
— l'odorat, m.	the smell	un col *ou*	
— le goût,	the taste	tour de cou,	a stock
— le toucher,	the feeling	un bonnet,	a cap
des engelures, f.	chilblains	bonnet de nuit,	a night cap
une brûlure,	a burn, a scald	une robe de chambre,	a morning or night gown
un rhume,	a cold		
une toux,	a cough	les bas, m.	the stockings
un mal-de-tête,	a headache	bas de laine,	worsted stockings
un mal de-gorge,	a sore throat	bas de coton,	cotton stockings
une dartre,	a tetter	bas de soie,	silk stockings
une verrue,	a wart	chaussettes, f.	under stockings

— 15 —

chaussons, m.	socks	
les jarretières, f.	the garters	
les pantoufles,	the slippers	
les souliers,	the shoes	
les escarpins,	the pumps	
les boucles, f.	the buckles	
boucles d'argent,	silver buckles	
boucles d'acier,	steel buckles	
les bottes,	the boots	
un tire-bottes,	boot-jack	
les éperons,	the spurs	
des guêtres,	spatterdashes	
une perruque,	a wig	
perruque à queue,	cue-wig	
perruque à bourse,	bag-wig	
perruque ronde,	round-wig	
perruque à l'abbé,	bob-wig	
un chapeau,	a hat	
chapeau uni,	plain hat	
chapeau galonné,	laced hat	
une cocarde,	a cockade	
un mouchoir,	a handkerchief	
un mouchoir de poche,	a pocket handkerchief	
un mouchoir de cou,	a neck handkerchief	
les gants, m.	the gloves	
gants de peau,	leather gloves	
gants de soie,	silk gloves	
une montre,	a watch	
montre d'or,	gold watch	
montre d'argent,	silver watch	
montre à répétition,	a repeating watch	
le cadran,	the dial plate	
l'aiguille, f.	the hour hand	
la boîte,	the case	
la chaîne,	the chain	
le cordon,	the string	
la clé ou clef,	the key	
le crochet,	the hook	
le cachet,	the seal	
une tabatière,	a snuff box	
une bague,	a ring	
une bourse,	a purse	
une lorgnette,	opera glass	
des lunettes.	spectacles	
une épée,	a sword	
le ceinturon,	the belt	
une canne,	a cane	
un bâton,	a stick	
une baguette,	a switch	
une houssine,	a twig	
un fouet,	a whip	

DES HABITS DE FEMMES.
Of the Women's Clothes.

une chemise de femme	}	a shift / a smock
une gorgerette un tour de gorge	}	a tucker
les manches, f.		the sleeves
manchettes, f.		ruffles
le corps,		the stays
un corset,		a bodice
des brassières, f.		jumps
un lacet,		a lace
un poinçon,		a bodkin
la pièce,		the stomacher
une échelle de rubans	}	a stomacher of ribbons
une jupe,		a petticoat
un jupon,		under-petticoat
jupon piqué,		quilted petticoat
un panier,		a hoop
un fourreau,		a frock
une robe,		a gown
robe de toile,		linen gown
robe de coton,		cotton gown
robe d'indienne,		calico gown
robe de soie,		silk gown
une écharpe,		a scarf
un tablier,		an apron
un mantelet,		a cloak
des mitaines, f.		mittens
une coiffure,		a head dress
une cornette,		a mob
un collier,		a necklace
un éventail,		a fan
des boucles d'oreilles,	}	ear-rings
des pendans d'oreilles,	}	drops or pendants
un anneau,		a plain ring
un jonc,		a hoop ring
un bracelet,		a bracelet
un bouquet,		a nosegay
des joyaux, m.		jewels
des diamans, m.		diamonds
un porte-feuille,		a pocket-book

SECT. VIII.
DES ALIMENTS ET DE LA BOISSON.
Of Food and Drink.

un pain,	a loaf
petit pain,	a roll
du pain,	some bread
pain blanc,	white bread
pain bis,	brown bread
pain frais,	new bread
pain rassis,	stale bread
de la mie,	some crumb
de la croute,	some crust
une tranche,	a slice
un morceau,	a bit, a morsel
une bouchée,	a mouthful
du bouillon,	some broth
de la soupe,	some soup
de la viande,	some meat
du bouilli,	boiled meat
du rôti,	roast meat
du bœuf,	some beef
du veau,	some veal
du mouton,	some mutton
de l'agneau,	some lamb
du porc,	some pork
du lard,	some bacon
du jambon,	some ham
des saucisses, f.	sausages
des trippes, f.	some tripe
une volaille,	a fowl
une poularde,	a pullet
du poisson,	some fish
de la sauce,	some sauce
un œuf,	an egg
du sel,	some salt
du poivre,	some pepper
de la muscade,	some nutmeg
de la moutarde,	some mustard
de l'huile,	some oil
du vinaigre,	some vinegar
du beurre,	some butter
beurre frais,	fresh butter
beurre salé,	salt butter
du fromage,	some cheese
un biscuit,	a biscuit
un gâteau,	a cake
un pâté,	a pie
des confitures,	sweetmeats
du sucre,	some sugar
un flan,	a custard
une tarte,	a tart
une talmouse,	a cheese-cake
de l'eau, f.	some water
du lait,	some milk
du petit lait,	some whey
de la crême,	some cream
de la bière,	some beer
bière forte,	strong-beer
du cidre,	some cider
du poiré,	some perry
du vin,	some wine
vin rouge,	red wine
vin blanc,	white wine
du thé,	some tea
thé bou,	bohea tea
thé vert,	green tea
du café,	some coffee
du chocolat,	some chocolate
de l'eau-de-vie,	some brandy

SECT. IX.
DES DIVERTISSEMENTS, &c.
Of Plays and Diversions.

Un jeu,	a game, a play
un passe-temps,	a pastime
un joujou,	a plaything
une balle,	a ball
un balon,	a foot ball
un volant,	a shuttle-cock
une raquette,	a racket
une toupie,	whirligig
un sabot,	a top
une corniche,	a gig
une lanière,	a lash
un cerceau,	a hoop
une crécelle,	a rattle
un bilboquet,	cup and ball
des marbres,	marbles
un sifflet,	a whistle
une canonnière,	a pop-gun
des échasses, f.	stilts
le frappe-main,	hot cockles
le coupe-tête,	leap frog
le colin-maillard,	blind man's buff
à pair ou non,	the game at even or odd
à croix ou pile,	the game at head or tail
le jeu de boules,	the game at bowls
le jeu de quilles,	the game at nine-pins
une boule,	a bowl
le but,	the jack at (bowls)

une quille,	a pin	une chienne,	a bitch
le jeu de barres,	the game of prison bars	un cochon,	a hog, a pig
		un daim,	a deer
le jeu de la fossette,	the game at chuck farthing	une daine,	a doe
		un écureuil,	a squirrel
la poussette,	push-pin	un furet,	a ferret
le jeu de la crosse,	the game at cricket	une génisse,	a heifer
		une jument,	a mare
une crosse,	a bat	un lapin,	a rabbit
un cerf-volant,	a kite	un lièvre,	a hare
une brandilloire,	a swing	un lion,	a lion
une balançoire,	a see-saw	un loup,	a wolf
un jeu de hasard,	a game of chance	un mouton,	a sheep
un jeu d'adresse,	a game of skill	un ours,	a bear
le jeu de paume,	the game at tennis	un poulain,	a colt
le jeu de billard,	the game billiards	un rat,	a rat
le jeu de dames,	the game of draughts	un renard,	a fox
		un sanglier,	a wild boar
un damier,	a draught-board	un singe,	a monkey
le jeu des échecs,	the game of chess	une souris,	a mouse
un échiquier,	a chess board	un taureau,	a bull
un jeu de cartes,	a pack of cards	une truie,	a sow
un atout or une triomphe,	a trump	une vache,	a cow
		un veau,	a calf
		un oiseau (o·a)	a bird
une main, une levée,	a trick	un aigle,	an eagle
		une alouette,	a lark
un jeton,	a counter	une bécasse,	a woodcock
une fiche,	a fish	une bécassine,	a snipe
des dés, m.	some dice	un canard,	a duck
		un chardonneret,	a goldfinch

SECT. X.

DES ANIMAUX ET DES OISEAUX.
Of Animals and Birds.

		un cigne,	a swan
		un coq,	a cock
		un corbeau,	a raven
		une corneille,	a crow
Un animal,	an animal	un dinde,	a turkey
un agneau,	a lamb	un faisan,	a pheasant
un âne,	an ass	une hirondelle,	a swallow
une belette,	a weasel	une linotte,	a linnet
un bélier,	a ram	un moineau,	a sparrow
une biche,	a hind	une oie,	a goose
un blaireau,	a badger	un paon, (pan)	a peacock
un bœuf,	an ox	une perdrix,	a partridge
un bouc,	a he-goat	un perroquet,	a parrot
une brebis,	an ewe	une pie,	a magpie
un cerf,	a stag	un pigeon,	a pigeon
un chat,	a cat	une poule,	a hen
une chatte,	a she-cat	un poulet,	a chicken
un cheval,	a horse	un rossignol,	a nightingale
des chevaux,	some horses	un serin,	a canary-bird
une chèvre,	a she-goat		
une chevreau,	a kid		
un chien,	a dog		

SECT. XI.

DES POISSONS ET DES INSECTES.

Of Fishes and Insects.

Un poisson,	a fish
une alose,	a shad
un anchois,	an anchovy
une anguille,	an eel
un barbeau,	a barbel
une barbue,	a dab
un brochet,	a pike, jack
une carpe,	a carp
un carrelet,	a flounder
une crevette,	a shrimp
une écrevisse,	a crawfish
écrevisse de mer,	a lobster
un éperlan,	a smelt
un goujon,	a gudgeon
un hareng,	a herring
une huître,	an oyster
une limande,	a burt, bret
un maquereau,	a mackerel
une melette,	a sprat
un merlan,	a whiting
une merluche,	a haddock
une morue,	a codfish
une moule,	a muscle
une perche,	a perch
une pétoncle,	a cockle
une plie,	a plaice
un rouget,	a roach
une sardine,	a pilchard
un saumon,	a salmon
une sole,	a soal, sole
une tanche,	a tench
une truite,	a trout
un turbot,	a turbot
un insecte,	an insect
une abeille,	a bee
une araignée,	a spider
un bourdon,	a drone
une cantharide,	a Spanish fly
un cerf-volant,	a horned beetle
une chenille,	a caterpillar
un ciron,	a hand-worm
un cloporte,	a wood-louse
un cousin,	a gnat
un crapaud,	a toad
un escarbot,	a beetle
une fourmi,	an ant
un frélon,	a hornet
une grenouille,	a frog
un grillon,	a cricket
une guêpe,	a wasp
un hanneton,	a cock chafer
un limaçon,	a snail
une limace,	a slug
une mouche,	a fly
un papillon,	a butterfly
un perce-oreille,	an ear-wig
un pou,	a louse
une puce,	a flea
une punaise,	a bug
une sangsue,	a leech
une sauterelle,	a grasshopper
un taon,	an ox-fly
un ver,	a worm
un vermisseau,	a small worm
un ver-à-soie,	a silk-worm
un ver-luisant,	a glow-worm
une vipère,	a viper

A LIST OF ADJECTIVES NOT FOUND IN GRAMMARS ALPHABETICALLY ARRANGED

Abattu, e.	faint, dejected	aimable,	{ amiable, agreeable / lovely, charming
abstême,	{ abstemious, one who drinks no wine	aise, glad, jouful, well pleased, happy	
absent, e.	absent	aisé, e.	{ easy, convenient, in easy circumstances
absolu, e.	absolute		
abstrait, e.	{ abstruse, inattentive, absent	alarmant, e.	dreadful, alarming
		alègre,	brisk, lively
absurde,	nonsensical, absurd	alerte,	{ cheerful, watchful, upon one's guard
accablant, e.	troublesome, very heavy		
acceptable,	{ acceptable, worth accepting	alisé or alizé, "les vents alisés,"	{ used only in the "trade winds"
accessible,	accessible	alité, e.	bed ridden
accommodant, e.	{ complaisant, complying	altéré, e.	thirsty, dry
		altier, e.	proud, haughty
accordable,	that may be granted	ambigu, e.	ambiguous, equivocal
acéphale,	without a head or chief	ambitieux, se.	ambitious
"statue acéphale",	{ a statue without a head	ambulant, e.	strolling, roving
		un comédien ambulant,	a strolling player
acide,	acid, sharp		
acrimonieux, se.	acrimonious	amer, e.	bitter
adorable,	adorable, divine	ami, e.	friendly, courteous
adoptif, ve.	adoptive	amiable,	kind, friendly
adoucissant, e.	emollient	à l'amiable,	{ amicably, in a friendly manner
adroit, e	skillful, dexterous		
adventif, ve.	adventitious, causal	amoureux, se.	{ in love, smitten, fond of, amorous
aérostatique,	{ concerning aerial navigation		
		ample,	large, wide, plentiful
affable,	courteous, affable	ampoulé, e.	bombastic, high-flown
affairé, e.	full of business	analogue,	analogous
affecté, e.	affected	ancien, ne.	ancient, of former times.
affectif, ve.	pathetic	angélique,	angelical
affectionné, e.	affectionate, loving	angulaire,	angular
affectueux, se.	full of kindness	"Pierre angulaire,"	Corner stone
"des manières affecteuses,"	kind manners	appétissant, e.	{ relishing, lovely, desirable
affidé, e.	trusty	ardent, e.	{ ardent, very hot, fierce, violent
affreux, se.	{ frightful, dreadful, shocking		
		ardoisé, e.	slate colored.
agaçant, e.	alluring, enticing	aride,	dry, barren, unfruitful
âgé, e.	aged, stricken in years	arqué, e.	bent like a bow, crooked
agent, e.	an agent	assuré, e.	{ sure, confident, bold, certain.
"agent de change", a stock broker			
aigre,	sour, shrill, sharp, severe	atroce,	atrocious, highly wicked
ailé, e.	winged	attaché, e.	covetous, near, selfish.
aimantin, e.	magnetic	atteint, e.	hit, struck, etc.
aîné, e.	{ eldest brother, m. eldest sister, f.	attenant, e.	contiguous
		atténuant, e.	mitigating, weakening

attractif, ve.	attractive	calme,	calm, quiet
attristant, e.	sad, afflicting	camus, e.	flat-nosed
auguste,	majestic, sacred, august	capable,	capable, able, etc.
avaricieux, se.	stingy, mean, covetous	capital, e.	capital, chief, principal
avarié, e.	damaged	carré, e.	square
avenant, e.	{ well-looking, genteel, suitable	central, e.	central
		cérémonieux, se.	ceremonious
aveugle,	blind	charitable,	charitable
avide,	greedy, eager	chaud, e.	warm, hot
aviné, e.	seasoned with wine	chauve,	bald
"C'est un corps aviné"	"He is a good toper"	cher, e.	dear
		chétif, ve.	mean, pitiful, poor
azuré, e.	of a blue color	choisi, e.	chosen, selected
"La voûte azurée,"	The azure sky	civil, e.	civil, political
Badin, e.	{ frolicksome, full of play, sportive	clair, e.	clear, bright, etc.
		clairvoyant, e.	{ discerning, clear sighted
basané, e.	tawny, sunburnt		
bas, se.	low, mean, dishonorable	classique,	classical
beau, bel, } belle	{ belle, beautiful, fine, handsome	comble,	heaped to the top
		comique,	comical
beni, e, ite.	praised, blessed	commercial, e.	commercial
bienvenu, e.	welcome	commode,	convenient, commodious
bienvoulu, e.	beloved, esteemed	commun, e.	common, usual, ordinary
bizarre,	capricious, fantastical	compact, e.	close, compact
bisulce,	cloven footed, (Nat. Hist.)	comparable,	comparable, suitable
		complaisant, e.	complaisant
blanc, che.	white	complet, e.	complete
blessé, e.	wounded	compliqué, e.	complicated
blond, e.	light, fair	compréhensible,	intelligible
bon, ne.	good, kind, etc.	compris, e.	comprehended
boréal, e.	northern	comptant, e.	ready
bossu, e.	hump-backed	"argent comptant",	ready money
bot, (pied)	club-footed	concerté, e. stiff, affected, agreed upon	
boiteux, se.	lame, limping	conciliable,	reconcilable
bouché, e.	heavy, dull, stopt	concis, e.	short, brief
boueux, se.	muddy, miry, dirty	concluant, e.	convincing, conclusive
bouffon, ne.	full of drollery	conditionné, e.	in good order
branlant, e.	shaking	confiant, e,	confiding
brief, ève.	short	confondu, e.	confounded, perplexed
brûlant, e.	hot, burning	conjugal, e.	conjugal
brûlé, e.	burnt	conséquent, e.	consistent
"vin brûlé",	mulled wine	considérable,	considerable
brun, e.	brown	considérant, e.	considerate, cautious
brut, e.	rough, unpolished	consolable,	consolable
brutal, e.	brutish, churlish, rude	contestable,	disputable
bruyant, e.	noisy	contraint, e.	constrained, stiff
Caduc, que.	decrepit, worn out	contraire,	{ contrary, hurtful, adverse, opposed
"le mal caduc,"	the falling sickness		
cagot, e.	hypocritical	contrariant, e.	{ of a contradictory temper
calleux, se.	callous, hardened		
calomnieux, se.	{ slanderous, calumnious	convenable,	{ convenient, proper, suitable, seasonable

coriace, as tough as leather
"un homme coriace," { a tough fisted fellow
corrigible, corrigible
courageux, se. { courageous, bold, resolute
couperosé, e. red, full of pimples
courant, e. { flowing, running current, present
court, e. short
"avoir la vue courte," { to be short sighted
cousu, e. sewed, stitched
couvert, e. covered
craintif, ve. timorous, fearful
creux, se. hollow, deep
criant, e. glaring, snameful
criard, e. clamorous, noisy
criminel, le. criminal, guilty
croupisssant, e. standing, stagnating
croyable, credile worthy of belief
cru, e. raw, crude, unmannerly
cruel, le. cruel, unkind, hardhearted
cursive, { used only in writing as "écriture cursive," a running hand
Dangereux, se. dangerous
dansant, e. dancing
débile, { debilitated, weak, feeble, faint
décent, e. becoming, decent
décidé, e. decided
décisif, ve. decisive, peremptory
déclinant, e. declining
défectueux. se. defective, faulty
délicat, e. delicate, fine, dainty
délicieux, se. delicious, voluptuous
délié, e. fine, thin, small
déloyal, e. disloyal, unfaithful
dénaturé, e. unnatural
dense, dense, close, compact
désastreux, se. disastrous, unfortunate
désavantageux, se. disadvantageous
désert, e. deserted
désirable, desirable
désolant, e. grievous, afflicting
désolé, e. disconsolable
despotique, despotical
détestable, { detestable, hateful, wretched
dévolu, e. devolved, transferred
dévot, e. devoted, bigoted

différent, e. distinct, diverse, various
difficile, hard, troublesome, difficult
diffus, e. prolix, diffuse
digne, { deserving, worthy, honest, upright
discorde, discord, strife
disgracieux, se. { ungraceful, disagreeable, disgraceful
discret, e. { discreet, prudent, considerate
divers, e. various, différent, remote
divin, e. divine, excellent
docile, docile, submissive
dodu, e. fat, plump
douloureux, se. painful, smarting
douteux, se. doubtful
doux, ce. soft, sweet
droit, e. right, just, honest, straight
dur, e. hard, firm
durable, lasting
Eblouissant, e. dazzling
échauffant, e. healing
échevelé, e. dishevelled
écumeux, se. frothy, foamy
efficace, efficacious, powerful
égaré, e. { strayed, wild, out of one's senses
égrillard, e. sprightly, mettlesome
éminent, e· high, lofty
endurant, e. { patient, who submits to insult
enfantin, e. childish
ennuyant, e. { wish causes weariness, tedious, tiresome
ennuyeux, se. { wearisome, tiresome, troublesome
enragé, e. desperate, mad, raging
entreprenant, e. { enterprising, bold, daring
envieux, se. envious
épais, se. thick, dense
épars, e. scattered, dispersed
éperdu, e. dismayed
épineux, se. difficult, thorny, prickly
éploré, e. all in tears, bathed in tears
équivoque, equivocal
errant, e, wandering
erroné, e. erroneous
érudit, e. learned, erudite
étonné, e. astonished

espiègle,	{ waggish, frolicsome, a little mischievous	"un fri-pon fieffé," fiévreux, se.	an arrant rogue feverish
éternel, le.	{ everlasting, without end, eternal	filial, e. fin, e.	filial cuning, fine, sly
étoilé, e.	starry	figuré, e.	figurative
étouffant, e.	sultry	finaud, e.	sly, artful
étrange,	strange, foreign	fixe,	immovable, steady
étroit, e.	narrow, strait	fluide,	fluid, liquid
évitable,	avoidable	foncé, e.	deep
exact, e.	ponctual, exact	"couleur foncée"	deep coloured
excellent, e.	excellent, rare	fondu, e.	melted
excessif, ve.	excessive	forcené, e.	mad
expérimenté, e.	experienced	formel, le.	formal
exprès, se.	express, plain, clear	fort, e.	strong, vigourous
expressif, ve.	expressive	fou, (fol) folle.	foolish, mad,
expiatoire,	expiatory	fragile	brittle, weak
exprimable,	that can be expressed	frais, che.	fresh, cool
extant, e.	extant, in being	franc, che.	frank, sincere, open
extérieur, e.	exterior, outward	fréquent, e.	frequent
externe,	external	frivole,	frivolous
extrait, e.	extracted	froid, e.	cold
Fabuleux, se.	fabulous	Gai, e.	cheerful
facétieux, se.	facetious, merry	gauche,	left, awkward
facile,	easy	généreux, se.	{ generous, liberal, magnanimous
fâcheux, se.	hard, provoking		
factice,	factitious, made, coined	gentil, le	genteel, neat, pretty
"un mot factice"	a new coined word	glaçant, e.	freezing
factieux, se.	factious, seditious	glacé, e.	frozen, glazed
faible,	weak	glissant, e.	slippery
fade,	insipid, nauseous	glorieux, se.	glorious
fainéant, e.	idle, lazy, slothful	gluant, e.	glutinous, tenacious
falot, e.	ridiculous	gracieux, se.	graceful, becoming
famé, e.	famed	graisseux, se.	greasy
famélique,	famished, starved	grand, e.	big, tall, great, huge
fameux, se.	famous	gratuit, e.	gratuitous
fantasque,	fantastical, whimsical	grave,	heavy, grave, low
farci, e.	stuffed	Grec, que.	Grecian, Greek
fardé, e.	painted, rouged	gredin, e.	beggarly, shabby
fatigué, e.	tired, fatigued	grièche,	speckled
fautif, ve.	faulty	grossier, e.	coarse, mean, vile
faux, sse.	false, deceitful	grotesque,	grotesque, ridiculous
favorable,	propitious, kind	gueux, se.	needy, indigent
favori, te.	agreeable, best, liked	"Il est gueux comme un rat d'église,"	{ "He is as poor as a church mouse"
fécond, e.	fruitful, prolific		
félon,	rebellious, cruel		
ferme,	fast, strong, steady	Habile,	skilful
fertile,	fertile	haut, (h. a.) e.	high, tall
feu, ue.	late, deceased,	heroïque,	heroical
"le feu roi,"	the late king	hideux, se.	hideous
"la feue reine"	the late queen	heureux, se.	happy, fortunate, lucky
fidèle,	faithful	homicide,	murderous, killing
fieffé, e.	arrant, downright	homogène,	homogeneous

honni, obsol,	confounded, abashed	indigne,	undeserving, unworthy
"Honni soit qui }	"Evil be to him,	indiscret, e.	indiscreet, unwise
mal y pense," }	that evil thinks"	indistinct, e.	indistinct, confused
honteux, se.	shameful, ashamed	individuel, le.	individual, single, particular
horrible, horrible,	frightful, dreadful		
humain, e.	humane, human	inexpiable,	not to be atoned for
humide,	wet, damp, humid	inédit, e,	unpublished
hydropique	dropsical	inexercé, e.	unexercised
hypocrite	hypocritical	inexorable,	inexorable, not to be entreated
Idiot, e.	silly, foolish		
ignorant, e.	ignorant,	infâme,	infamous, base
ignoble,	ignoble, vile, base	infertile,	unfruitful, barren
ignomineux, se.	{ ignominous, disgraceful	infirme,	infirm, weak, sickly
		infortuné, e.	unfortunate, unhappy, unlucky
illégitime,	illegitimate, unjust		
imbu, e.	imbued, tinctured	ingénieux, se,	ingenious, witty dexterous, skillful
immense,	immense		
immobile	immovable	ingénu, e.	frank, sincere, without [guile
immodéré, e.	immoderate		
immortel, e.	immortel	ingrat, e.	ungrateful
impair,	odd	intelligent, e.	intelligent
"nombre impair"	"odd number"	intègre,	upright, honest
impatient, e.	impatient	intarissable,	that never dries up
impérieux, se.	imperious	intrépide,	fearless, undaunted
impétueux, se.	impetuous, hasty	intestat, e.	intestate, dying without a will
impoli, e.	impolite		
important, e	important	introuvable,	not to be found
imprévoyant, e.	improvident	inutile,	useless
imprévu, e.	unforeseen	invendu, e.	unsold
improbable,	improbable	inversable,	{ (of a carriage) cannot be overset
impuni, e.	unpunished		
impropre,	improper		
impudent, e.	impudent	isolé, e.	insulated, alone
impur, e	impure	issu, e.	sprung, descended
incapable,	incapable, unfit	ivre,	inebriated, intoxicated
incertain, e.	uncertain,	"ivre mort,"	"dead drunk"
incivil, e.	uncivil, doubtful	jaloux, se.	jealous, envious, tender
incommode,	troublesome, incon- [venient	jambé, e.	legged
		jeune,	young, fiery
inconnu, e.	unknown, strange	joli, e.	pretty, neat, bonny
inconstant, e.	inconstant	joufflu, e.	chubcheeked, chubby
incorrect, e.	incorrect	journalier, e.	daily, uncertain
incorruptible,	incorruptible	"Les armes sont journalières,"	{ "The fate or chance of war is uncertain"
incroyable,	incredible		
indécis, e.	undecided, irresolute		
indéfendu, e.	defenceless	jovial, e.	jovial, merry
indéfini, e.	indefinite	joyeux, se.	joyous, glad
indélicat, e.	indelicate	Juif, ve.	Jewish
indevot, e.	irreligious	juste, /	just, equitable, lawful
indicible,	unspeakable	justificatif, ve.	serving to prove
indifférent, e.	indifferent	juteux, se.	juicy
indigeste,	indigestible	laborieux, se.	laborious

lâche,	slack, sluggish, cowardly	malhonnête,	{ dishonest, rude, uncivil, knavish
ladre,	leprous, stingy, mean		
laid, e.	ugly, plain	malicieux, se.	malicious, wicked
laiteux, se.	milky	malpropre,	uncleanly, slovenly
langoureux, se.	languishing, drooping, lingering	maniéré, e.	affected
		"manière noire,"	"mezzotinto"
languissant, e.	languid, weak, faint	manifeste,	manifest, plain
lanifère,	bearing wool, lanigerous	marri, e.	sorry, grieved
lanugineux, se.	downy, lanuginous	mauvais, e	bad, evil, ill
large,	broad, wide, large	médisant, e.	slanderous, reviling
larmoyant, c.	in tears, pathetic, moving	méfiant, e.	mistrustful
		mémoratif, ve.	remembering
las, se.	weary, tired	méridional, e.	southern
léger, c.	light, active	méritoire,	worthy of being rewarded
lent, e.	slow, sluggish, dull	mielleux, se.	that tasted like honey
libertin, e.	libertine, licentious, irreligious	miraculeux, se	miraculous
		moisi, e	mouldy, hoary
libre,	free, at liberty	mollet, te.	a little soft
limoneux, se.	muddy, slimy, oozy, marshy	mondain, e.	wordly
		montagneux, se.	mountainous, hilly
livide,	black and blue, livid	mort, e.	dead
lointain, e.	far away, distant	morose,	morose, sad
long, ue.	long	mortel, le.	deadly, mortal
louable,	praiseworthy, laudable	muet, te.	dumb, speechless
louche,	squint, looking awry	mucilagineux, se.	mucilaginous
loupeux, se	knobby	musical, e.	musical
"un arbre loupeux,"	a knobby tree	mutin, e.	mutinous
lourd, e.	heavy	mystérieux, se.	mysterious
loyal, e.	loyal, faithful, trusty	naïf, ve.	{ natural, unaffected ingenuous
lucide,	lucid, bright		
lucratif, ve.	{ lucrative, gainful, profitable	nain, e.	dwarfish
		naissant, e.	{ rising, coming forth beginning to appear
lugubre,	mournful, sad		
luisant, e.	bright, shining	naturel, le.	natural, unaffected
"un ver luisant,"	"a glow worm"	natal, e.	natal
lumineux, se	{ luminous, emitting light	natif, ve.	native born
		"il est natif de Berlin,"	{ he was born in Berlin
lunaire,	lunar, lunary	nébuleux, se.	nebulous
"rayons lunaires,"	"moon beams"	nécessaire,	necessary
maigre,	meagre, lean	nécessiteux,	needy, necessitous
majestueux, se.	majestic	négligent, e.	negligent
malade,	ill, sick	nerveux, se.	nervous, sinewy
maladif, ve.	sickly, unhealthy	net, te.	clean, neat
mâle,	stout, manly	neuf, ve.	new, fresh
maléfique,	mischievous	niais, se.	silly, foolish, simple
malfait, e.	{ ill made, badly done, ill shaped	noir, e.	black, dark
		"un noir chagrin,"	a gloomy sorrow
malgracieux, se.	{ unmannerly ungracious	nonpareil, le.	matchless, incomparable
malhabile,	unskillful		
malheureux, se.	unhappy, unlucky unfortunate	nouveau nouvel, le.	} new

— 25 —

non pair,	odd
novice,	inexperienced
nu, e.	naked
nuageux, se.	cloudy
nubile,	marriageable
nutritif, ve.	nutritious
obligeant, e.	civil, kind, accommodating, obliging
obscur, e.	gloomy, dark
obstiné, e.	obstinate, stubborn
odieux, se.	odious, hateful
œuvré,	(said of fishes) hard-roed
offensant, e.	offensive
officieux, se.	kind, obliging
oisif, ve.	idle, useless
olivâtre,	of an olive colour
ombrageux, se.	suspicious
onctueux, se.	oily, clammy
ondoyant, e.	undulating, waving
opiniâtre,	obstinate
opulent, e.	rich, opulent
orageux, se.	tempestuous, stormy
ordinaire,	ordinary, common
orgueilleux, se.	proud, haughty
originaire,	originally, coming from
original, e.	original, first
ossu, e.	bony
ouvert, e.	open
ouvré, e.	(said of linen) diapered, worked
Paissant, e	grazing
pâle,	pale
pantois, e.	short-winded
paradoxial, e.	paradoxical
pareil, le.	alike, equal
paresseux, se.	idle, lazy
parlant, e.	speaking
pâteux, se	mealy, gluish, sticky
pathétique	pathetical
paternel, le	paternal
patient, e.	patient
pen-lable,	that deserves hanging
perfide,	perfidious, false
périlleux, se.	perilous, dangerous
périssable,	perishable
permanent, e.	permanent, durable, lasting
perplexe,	perplexing, wavering, uncertain
pervers, e.	bad, wicked
la fortune perverse,	adverse fortune
petit, e.	small, little
pesant, e.	heavy, weighty slow, indolent
pétreux, se.	stony, gravelly
pétulant, e.	pert, saucy
peureux, se	timorous, fearful
pieux, se.	pious
piquant, e.	striking, tart, sharp
pitoyable,	pitiful, compassionate
plaintif, ve.	plaintive, complaining
plaisant, e.	pleasant, delightful, agreeable, merry
plat, e.	insipid, flat
plein, e.	full, replete
pluviale,	rainy, joined to
eau pluviale,	rainy water
poignant, e.	sharp, severe
pointilleux, se.	captious, cavelling
pointu, e.	pointed, sharp
portatif, ve.	portable
possible,	possible
poudreux, se.	powdery, dusty
préalable,	previous
précis, e.	precise
précieux, se.	precious
préliminaire,	previous
préfixe,	prefixed
prématuré, e.	too early premature
prédial, e.	predial
des rentes prédiales,	ground rents
préférable,	preferable
préjudiciable,	prejudicial
prenable,	that can be taken
préparatif, ve.	preparative
présent, e.	present
pressé, e.	in haste, in a hurry
prêt, e.	ready, prepared
prétendu, e.	pretended, self dubbed
prétentieux, se.	affected, pedantic
prévenant, e.	obliging, pleasing, valiant
preux, se,	
un preux chevalier,	a valiant knight
prévoyant,	forecasting, provident
probable,	probable, likely
prodigieux, se.	prodigious, amazing
prodigue,	prodigal, wasteful
profond, e.	deep
propre,	fit, becoming, apt
provenant, e.	coming, proceeding
puéril, e.	childish
puissant, e.	powerful, potent
pur, e.	pure, unmingled, guiltless

purpurin, e.	purplish	roulant, e.		rolling
putatif, ve.	supposed reputed	rude,		harsh, rough, severe
putride,	rotten, putrid	ruminant, e.		ruminating, chewing the cud
Quarte,	quartan			
la fièvre quarte,	the quartan ague	Sablonneux, se.		sandy
quinteux, se.	capricious, humorsome	sacrilège,		sacrilegious
quotidien, ne.	daily	sage,		(speaking of a man) wise, prudent
C'est son pain quotidien,	It is his daily custom	sage,		(of a femelle) modest
Raboteux, se.	rough, rugged	sage,		(of a child) good, sedate
rachitique,	ricketty	sage,		(of an animal) mild, tame
radieux, se.	radiant, shining	saint, e.		saint, holy, pious
raffiné, e.	clever, fine, keen	saisissant, e.		striking
raide,	stiff, rigid	un froid saisissant,		a striking cold
Il tomba raide mort,	He dropped down stone dead	sain, e.		healthy
		sale,		dirty, nasty
rampant, e.	creeping, crawling	salé, e,		salted
rapide,	swift, rapid	salubre,		salubrious, healthy
rare,	scarce, uncommon	salutaire,		safe, secure
ras, e.	smooth, plain	savonneux, se.		soapy
rebelle,	rebellious	séant, e.		sitting, decent
rébutant, e.	repulsive, displeasing	sec, che.		dry, barren, sandy
récent, e.	recent	secret, e.		secret, hidden
rechigné, e.	sour, crabbed	séditieux, se.		seditious, turbulent, factious
mine rechignée,	a sour look			
réciproque,	reciprocal, mutual	semblable,		like, alike
recuit, e.	overboiled	sérieux, se.		serious, solemn, grave
cela est cuit et recuit,	that is boiled to rags	séreux, se.		thin, watery
		sensible,		sensible, feeling
réductible,	reducible	serein, e.		clear, serene
réel, le.	real, true, genuine	serré, e.		close, compact
regardant, e.	too saving, niggardly	seul, e.		alone, only
régnant, e.	reigning	sévère,		severe
regrettable,	lamentable	signalé, e.	famous, signal, memorable
réjoui, e.	joyous	silencieux, se.		silent, still
religieux, se.	religious, pious	similaire,		similar, homogeneous
remuant,	stirring, moving	simple,		simple, plain
renommé, e.	renowned, famed	simultané, e.		simultaneous
réparable,	reparable	simulé, e.		deceitful, fictitious
répulsif, ve.	repulsive	sincère,		honest, sincere
réservé, e.	prudent, cautious	sobre,		temperate, sober
résineux, se.	resinous	soigneux, se.		careful, diligent
revenant, e.	likely, taking	solennel, le.		solemn, in due time
une physionomie revenante	a pleasing countenance	solitaire,		solitary, lonely
		sombre,		dark, gloomy
révoltant, e.	scandalous	somptueux, se.		sumptuous
riche,	rich, wealthy	soudain, e.		suddenly, immediately
ridé, e.	wrinkled	soûl, e.		full, glutted
rond, e.	round, circular	soumis, e.		submissive
rouge	red	soupçonneux, se.		suspicious
devenir rouge,	to blush	souterrain,		subterraneous
rougeâtre,	reddish	spacieux, se.		spacious

studieux, se.	studious	Vacillant, e.	reeling, staggering, tottering, wavering
suffocant, e.	stifling, choaking		
sujet, te.	subject, exposed	vague,	loose, indefined
superflu, e.	superfluous	vacant, e.	vacant
supérieur, u.	superior	vain, e.	vain, fruitless
sûr, e.	sure, certain	valeureux, se.	valiant, stout, courageous
surnaturel, le.	supernatural		
Tacheté, e.	speckled	valide,	legal, valid
tardif, ve.	tardy, slow, late	vaporeux, se.	vaporous
tarissable,	that can be dried up	veillant, e.	awake
tédieux, se.	tedious	vénéneux, se.	venomous
tel, le.	such	véreux, se.	full of maggots, rotten
téméraire,	bold, rash	vert, e.	green, fresh
tempestueux, se.	stormy, tempestuous	vertueux, se.	virtuous
		vêtu, e.	clad, dressed
tendre,	tender, soft	vide,	empty, void
terreux, se.	full of earth	vif, ve.	lively
têtu, e.	obstinate, headstrong	vicieux, se.	vicious, wicked
tortu, e.	crooked	vieux, vieil, eille	old, aged
tortueux, se.	winding		
touchant, e.	moving, affecting	victorieux, se,	victorious
touffu, e.	thick, bushy, tufted	vigoureux, se.	vigorous, stout
tourbeux, se.	turfy	vil, e.	vile, mean
tourmentant, e.	tormenting, troublesome	violent, e.	violent, passionate
		viril, e.	manly
tout, e.	all, every, any	vîte,	quick, swift
tranchant, e.	sharp, cutting	volant, e.	flying
triomphant, e.	victorious, triumphant	volage,	fickle, inconstant
		volatile,	flying, volatile
trivial, e.	trivial, common	volontaire.	voluntary, wilful
turbulent, e.	turbulent, violent	voluptueux, se.	voluptuous
tyrannique,	tyrannical	vomitif, ve.	vomitive
Uligineux, se.	damp, marshy	voyant, e.	very gaudy
unanime,	unanimous	vrai, e.	true, right, real
unique,	only, sole	vraisemblable,	likely, probable
usé, e.	worn out, used	vulgaire,	vulgar, common
utile,	useful, profitable	Zélé, e,	jealous, ardent, passionate

VERBES FRANÇAIS ET ANGLAIS
FRENCH AND ENGLISH VERBS.

Abaisser,	to lower, to humble, to let down
abandonner,	to forsake, to leave
abattre,	to pull down, to fell
abîmer,	to destroy, to ruin
abonner,	to compound
aboutir,	to border upon, to meet, to end in
abreuver,	to soak, to lead animals to drink
absoudre,	to absolve
accélérer,	to hasten
accepter,	to receive, to accept
accompagner,	to accompany
accoucher,	to deliver
acheminer,	to set forward
acquérir,	to acquire
adoniser;	to dress one's self out
adresser,	to direct a letter, to send, to dedicate
affecter,	to affect
aggraver,	to aggravate
agrandir,	to enlarge, to widen
aider,	to help, to assist
aigrir,	to exasperate, to make sour
aiguiser,	to sharpen
aimer,	to love, to like, to be fond of
ajuster,	to adjust, to fit up
alarmer,	to alarm
allumer,	to light, to kindle
aller,	to go
altérer,	to change
amarrer,	to moor a ship
amasser,	to gather, to collect
annoncer,	to announce
Badiner,	to joke
bâiller,	to gape, to yawn
baiser,	to kiss
bassiner,	to warm a bed
bâtir,	to build, to erect
battre,	to beat
bercer,	to rock a child
beugler,	to bellow
beurrer,	to butter
bigarrer,	to spreckle
blanchir, v. a.	to bleach linen, to wash linen
blanchir, v. n.	to grow white, to grow old
blesser,	to hurt, to wound
boucher,	to stop a hole, to block up
brûler,	to burn
Cacher,	to hide, to conceal
cadrer,	to suit, to agree, to answer
calomnier,	to calumniate
canarder,	to shoot at a person from a sheltered place
causer, v. n.	to prattle, to tattle
causer, v. a.	to cause, to occasion
céder,	to yield, to give up
célébrer,	to celebrate
ceindre,	to gird
chanter,	to sing
charger,	to charge, to load
chasser,	to drive away
chauffer,	to warm, to heat
choisir,	to choose, to select
clouer,	to nail
commencer,	to begin
concerner,	to belong, to concern
concerter,	to contrive, to agree
confondre,	to confound
connaître,	to know, to be acquainted with
conseiller,	to advise, to counsel
convoiter,	to covet
coudre,	to sew
couler,	to flow
courir,	to run
couvrir,	to cover
cracher,	to spit
creuser,	to dig, to deepen
croire,	to believe, to credit
cuire,	to cook, to bake
Débarrasser,	to rid, to get clear of a troublesome person
déborder,	to overflow, to jut out
décacheter,	to unseal
déchiffrer,	to decipher, to unravel
découvrir,	to uncover, to discover
décréter,	to order, to decree
défaillir,	to get weak, to fail
dégager,	to redeem
dégénérer.	to degenerate

dégrader,	to degrade	friser,	to curl hair
dégraisser,	to scour, to skim	fuser,	to melt
déloger,	to dislodge	Gagner,	to win, to gain, to earn
demeurer,	to dwell, to remain	garantir,	to warrant
dépêcher,	to dispatch, to send	garder,	to watch, to keep
dépeupler,	to depopulate	gargouiller,	to paddle in the water
dépoter,	to take a plant out of a pot	gémir,	to groan, to moan
		glacer,	to freeze, to chill
désassocier,	to dissolve partnership	glisser,	to slide, to slip
desserrer,	to loosen	glousser,	to cluck like a hen
desservir,	to clear the table	grandir,	to grow, to grow tall
dévorer,	to devour	griller,	to broil
différer,	to delay, to put off	guider,	to guide
disposer,	to dispose	Haïr, (*H. asp.*)	to hate
dorer,	to gild	haler,	to heave, to haul
doubler,	to double	hanter,	to haunt, to frequent
ébranler,	to shake, to move	hâter,	to hasten
ébruiter,	to divulge	hérisser,	to stand on end
écaler,	to shell	heurter,	to strike, to hit
écarter,	to drive away	hisser,	to hoist
échapper,	to escape	honnir,	to disgrace, to curse
échauder	to scald	houer,	to hoe
échauffer,	to heat, to warm	haranguer,	to make a speech
éclaircir,	to clear, to brighten	hurler,	to howl, to yell
échouer,	to fail, to run aground	habiller, (*H. mute*)	to dress
éclairer,	to light, to watch, to have an eye upon	hériter,	to inherit
		honorer,	to honor
écrire,	to write	humecter,	to moisten
égaliser,	to equalize	humilier,	to humiliate
égorger,	to cut the throat, to murder, to slaughter	Idolâtrer,	to idolize, to worship
		imaginer,	to imagine
égratigner,	to scratch	impliquer,	to implicate
embraser,	to burn, to consume by fire	impugner,	to impugn, to oppose
		imputer,	to ascribe, to attribute
embrasser,	to embrace, to hug	incarcérer,	to imprison
emporter,	to carry away	indemniser,	to indemnify
endosser,	to put on, to endorse	indiquer,	to indicate
Façonner,	to figure, to shape	inscrire,	to inscribe
fâcher,	to grieve, to afflict	intriguer,	to intrigue
farcir,	to stuff, to cram	Jaillir,	to spout out
feindre,	to hesitate, to scruple	japper,	to yelp, to bark
féliciter,	to congratulate	jeûner,	to fast
feuilleter,	to turn over the leaves	jouer,	to play
fiancer,	to betroth	jouir,	to enjoy
fixer,	to fix, to make firm	jucher,	to roost
flatter,	to flatter	juguler,	to choak
fondre,	to melt, to liquefy	justifier,	to justify
former,	to form	Labourer,	to till, to plough
fortifier,	to fortify	lacer,	to lace
fraîchir,	to freshen	laisser,	to leave
fréquenter,	to visit often	languir,	to languish
frire,	to fry	lever, v. a.	to lift, to raise

lever, v. n.	to grow, to grow up	peupler,	to populate
lier,	to tie, to bind	pincer,	to pinch
livrer,	to deliver, to give up	piler,	to pound
loucher,	to squint	plaindre,	to pity
louer,	to praise	plaire,	to please
lutter,	to wrestle, to struggle	pleuvoir,	to rain
Maigrir,	to grow lean	plonger,	to plunge, to dip
malfaire,	to do harm	plumer,	to pluck out feathers
mander,	to order, to acquaint with	poignarder,	to stab
manquer,	to fail	policer,	to govern, to civilize
marchander,	to bargain	polir,	to polish
marcher,	to march	pondre,	to lay eggs
marier,	to marry	porter,	to carry
masquer,	to disguise	poser,	to lay, to set, to put
mêler,	to mix, to mingle	postuler,	to put up for, to be a candidate for
menacer,	to threaten		
ménager,	to husband, to take care	pouiller,	to call names
modifier,	to modify	pourrir,	to putrefy
monter,	to mount, to ascend	pourvoir,	to provide
mortifier,	to mortify	prêcher,	to preach
mouiller,	to moisten, to wet	précipiter,	to precipitate
munir,	to store, to provide	prendre,	to take
Nager,	to swim	prêter,	to lend
naître,	to be born	prévenir,	to prevent, to prepossess
natter,	to mat	priver,	to deprive
négocier,	to negotiate	prohiber,	to prohibit
noircir,	to blacken	projeter,	to scheme, to contrive
nommer,	to name	protéger,	to protect
Obéir,	to obey	punir,	to punish
obliger,	to oblige	Quérir, (used only with aller,) to fetch	
offenser,	to offend	questionner,	to question
offrir,	to offer	quêter,	to beg, to collect money
ondoyer,	to rise in waves	quitter,	to quit
orner,	to ornament	Rabattre,	to pull down again
ôter,	to remove, to take off	racommoder,	to mend, to patch
ourdir,	to contrive, to warp	raccourcir,	to shorten
oublier,	to forget	racheter,	to buy again, to redeem
ouvrir,	to open	radoucir,	to soften
Pacifier,	to pacify	railler,	to jest, to jeer
pâlir,	to turn pâle	raisonner,	to argue, to reason
panser,	to dress a wound	ramasser,	to take up, to pick up
panser,	to look after a horse	rajeunir,	to grow young again
paraître,	to appear	rajuster,	to set in order again
parier,	to bet	ramer,	to row
partir,	to set out, to depart	ramoner,	to sweep a chimney
passer,	to pass, to call	ranger,	to set in order
payer,	to pay	râper,	to grate, to rasp
peindre,	to paint	rapprendre,	to learn again
penser,	to think	raser,	to shave
perfectionner,	to make perfect	rassurer, to quiet one's fear, to secure	
périr,	to perish	ratiser,	to poke the fire up
persécuter,	to persecute	rattraper, to catch again, to overtake	

ravager,	to ruin, to lay waste
recéler,	to conceal
réciter,	to recite
reconnaître,	to know again, to recognize
récréer,	to revive, to relieve, to delight, to refresh
recueillir,	to gather, to receive, to collect
reculer,	to recoil, to fall back
redire,	to say again, to repeat
redoubler,	to reiterate
réduire,	to reduce
réfléchir,	to reflect
régir,	to govern, to rule
régler,	to regulate
régner,	to reign
regretter,	to regret
rehausser,	to raise, to heighten
reléguer,	to exile
remédier,	to remedy
remercier,	to thank, to return thanks
remettre,	to restore, to remit
rendormir,	to fall asleep again
réparer,	to repare, to restore
répéter,	to repeat
reprendre,	to find fault, to take again
retenir,	to retain, to withhold
rêver,	to dream
revenir,	to return, to come again
rire,	to laugh
saccager,	to sack, to pillage, to plunder
saigner,	to bleed
saper,	to sap, to undermine
savoir,	to know
secourir,	to assist, to succour
séduire,	to seduce
seller,	to saddle
sentir,	to feel
serrer,	to serve, to attend
siffler,	to whistle
sommeiller,	to slumber, to doze
sommer,	to summon
sonner,	to ring, to strike, to sound
souffler,	to blow
souffrir,	to suffer
souiller,	to stain, to soil
soumettre,	to subdue
soutenir,	to sustain
subir,	to undergo, to submit
suer,	to perspire
suivre,	to follow
supplier,	to implore, to supplicate
surcharger,	to overload
survivre,	to survive, to outlive
sympathiser,	to sympathise
Tailler,	to cut, to carve
tarder,	to delay
tarir,	to drain, to dry up
taxer,	to tax
tenir,	to hold
têter,	to suck
tirer,	to draw, to pull
tolérer,	to tolerate
tomber,	to fall
tordre,	to twist, to wring
tortuer,	to make crooked
tourner,	to turn, to move round
traire,	to milk
traiter,	to treat, to settle
tranquilliser,	to tranquillize
travailler,	to work
trébucher,	to stumble, to tumble
trembler,	to tremble
tremper,	to dip, to steep
tricher,	to cheat
trotter,	to trot
tuer,	to kill
Unir,	to unite
user,	to wear out, to use
usurper,	to usurp
utiliser,	to make useful
Valoir,	to be worth
végéter,	to vegetate
veiller,	to watch, to sit up at night
vendre,	to sell
venir,	to come
vêtir,	to clothe
vider,	to empty
vieillir,	to grow old
violer,	to violate, to transgress
vivre,	to live
voguer,	to row
"Vogue la galère,"	"Let happen what may"
voiler,	to veil
voir,	to see
voler,	to fly, to steal
voyager,	to travel
vouloir,	to wish, to be willing

EXPRESSIONS QUI SONT INVARIABLES

*Expressions which are Invariable.**

Autrefois,	formerly	ici près,	just by
auparavant,	before	près d'ici,	hard by
dernièrement,	lately	là, de là,	there, from thence
aujourd'hui,	to-day	là haut,	above
à présent	at present	là bas,	below
maintenant	now	d'en haut,	from above
dans peu,	shortly	d'en bas,	from below
désormais,	hereafter	en dedans,	within
très-souvent,	very often	en dehors,	without
toujours,	always	sur, dessus,	upon, on
rarement,	seldom	sous, dessous,	under
quelquefois	sometimes	plus, moins,	more, less
jamais,	never, ever	de plus.	moreover
à jamais,	for ever	du moins,	at least
ailleurs,	elsewhere	surtout,	above all
d'ailleurs,	besides	tout au plus,	at the most
néanmoins,	nevertheless	sérieusement,	seriously
pourtant,	however	ensemble,	together
tôt ou tard.	soon or late	ensuite,	afterwards
bientôt	very soon	tour-à-tour,	by turns
trop tôt	too soon	oui vraiment,	yes indeed
trop tard,	too late	non—non pas,	no—not
trop peu,	too little	point du tout,	not at all
peu à peu,	little by little	pourquoi	why
encore,	again	parce que,	because
pas encore,	not yet	où, d'où,	where, from whence
ici, d'ici,	here, from hence		

---

* The following expressions and the like, which are frequently used to make the tenses of our Form of Speech either more clear, or better connected together, are called *invariable*, because they do not admit of a diversity of grammatical terminaisons, as those of the preceding Sections.

PHRASES FAMILIERES,

ET

Propres à exercer les Jeunes Gens dans la langue Française.

1.

Mon cher, m. ma chère, f.
Mon cher enfant, m. }
Ma chère enfant, f. }
Mon bel ange,
Mon amour,
Ma chère âme,
Mon cher Monsieur,
Ma chère Dame,

2.

Donnez-moi, s'il vous plait,
Une tasse de thé — de café,
Une beurrée,
De la crême ou du lait,
Un peu de sucre,
Je vous remercie,
Je vous rends grâces,

3.

Apportez-moi,
Mon livre — du papier,
De l'encre — une plume,
Prêtez-moi, pour un moment,
Un Dictionnaire,
Votre crayon — votre canif,
Je vous suis bien obligé,

4.

Accordez-moi une grâce,
Je vous prie,
Je vous supplie,
De tout mon cœur,
Si je le puis faire,
Permettez-moi de sortir,
Je ne saurais, Je ne puis pas,
Restez ici un moment,
Prenez votre ouvrage,

1.

My dear.
My dear child.

My pretty angel.
My love.
My dear soul.
My dear sir.
My dear madam.

2.

Give me if you please.
A cup of tea — of coffee.
A slice of bread and butter.
Some cream or some milk.
A bit of sugar.
I thank you.
I return you thanks.

3.

Bring me.
My book — some paper.
Some ink — a pen.
Lend me, for a moment.
A Dictionary.
Your pencil — yonr pen-knifer.
1 am greatly obliged to you.

4.

Grant me a favor.
Pray, or 1 pray you.
I beseech you or entreat you.
With all my heart.
If I can do it.
Give me leave to go out.
I cannot.
Stay here a moment.
Take up your work.

5.

Approchez-vous de moi,	Come near me.
Montrez-moi cela,	Show me that.
Asseyez-vous là,	Sit down there.
Prenez-garde,	Take care.
Préparez votre leçon,	Get your lesson ready.
Etes-vous prêt, m. prête ? f.	Are you ready ?
Je sais ma leçon,	I can say my lesson.
Levez-vous à présent,	Rise or get up now.
Fermez la porte,	Shut the door.
Ouvrez la fenêtre,	Open the window.
Allez vous chauffer,	Go and warm yourself.

6.

Que souhaitez-vous ?	What do you want ?
Que cherchez-vous ?	What do you look for ?
Qu'avez-vous perdu ?	What have you lost ?
Répondez-moi,	Answer me.
Je cherche mon chapeau,	I am looking for my hat.
Que dites-vous ?	What do you say ?
Parlez plus haut,	Speak louder.
Je ne vous entends pas,	I don't hear you.
A quoi pensez-vous ?	What are you thinking of ?
Que faites-vous ?	What are you doing ?
Qu'avez-vous fait ?	What have you done ?

I.

POUR ABORDER ET SALUER QUELQU'UN.

Of Meeting and Saluting a Person.

Monsieur, Madame, ou Mademoiselle,* je vous souhaite le bonjour,	Sir, madam, or miss, I wish you a good day, or good morning to you.
Comment vous portez-vous ce matin ?	How do you do this morning ?
Très-bien, Dieu merci,	Very well, thank God.
Je me porte fort bien,	I am very well.
A votre service,	At your service.
Prêt à vous rendre service,	Ready to serve you.
Et vous, comment va la santé ?	And you, how is it with you ?
Assez-bien,	Pretty well.
Passablement bien,	Tolerably well.
Tout doucement; là là,	Indifferent; so so.
A mon ordinaire,	As usual.
Parfaitement bien,	Exceedingly well.
J'en suis bien-aise,	I am very glad of it.
Et vous, Madame, comment va l'état de votre santé ?	And you, madam, how do you enjoy your health ?
Je ne me porte pas bien,	I am not well.
J'en suis fâché, m. fâchée, f.	I am sorry for it.

* Although I have omitted inserting either of these three titles, *Monsieur, etc.* in following phrases, yet one of them is to be used according to the person spoke to, every time a question or an answer is made.

Comment se porte monsieur votre frère aujourd'hui ?	How does your brother do to-day ?
Il est un peu indisposé,	He is a little indisposed.
Il est enrhumé; il a mal à la tête,	He has a cold; he has the head-ache.
Je suis fâché d'apprendre qu'il se porte mal,	I am sorry to hear he is ill.
J'irai le voir ce soir,	I'll go and see him this evening.

II.

DU TEMPS ET DE L'HEURE.
Of the Weather and the Hour.

Quel temps fait-il ?	What weather is it ?
Fait-il beau temps ?	Is it fine weather ?
Fait-il froid ou chaud ?	Is it cold or hot ?
Il fait un temps clair, serein et sec,	It is clear, serene, and dry weather.
—obscur, humide, venteux, orageux, pluvieux,	—dark, wet, windy, stormy weather.
Pleut-il ? Neige-t-il ?	Does it rain ? Does it snow ?
Il pleut à verse,	It rains very hard.
Il neige un peu,	It snows a little.
Il gèle—il grêle,	It freezes—it hails.
Il fait grand vent,	The wind is very high.
Il fait un brouillard fort épais,	There is a very thick fog.
Le soleil commence à paraître,	The sun begins to appear.
Je vois l'arc-en-ciel,	I see the rainbow.
C'est signe de beau temps,	It is a sign of fair weather.
Quelle heure est-il ?	What o'clock ?
Il n'est pas tard,	It is not late.
Il est près d'une heure,	It is almost one o'clock.
Une heure vient de sonner,	It has just struck one.
Il est une heure et demie,	It is half an hour past one.
Il s'en va deux heures,	It is almost two o'clock.
L'horloge sonne,	The clock strikes.
Deux heures sont sonnées,	It has struck two.
Je ne croyais pas qu'il fût si tard,	I did not think it was so late.
Regardez à votre montre,	Look at your watch.
Elle avance—elle retarde,	It goes too fast—it goes too slow.
Elle ne va pas bien,	It does not go right.

III.

POUR ALLER, VENIR & ETC.
Of Going, Coming & etc.

Où allez vous?	Where are you going?
Je vais chez-nous,	I am going home.
D'où venez-vous?	Whence do you come?
Je viens de chez M. B—	I come from Mr. B—'s.
Voulez-vous venir avec moi?	Will you go along with me?
Voulez-vous faire un tour?	Will you take a walk?
Répondez-moi; dites-moi oui ou non,	Answer me; tell me yes or no.
Je n'ai pas le temps,	I have no time.
Je le veux bien; j'y consens,	I will; I consent to it.
Où irons-nous?	Where shall we go?
Par où irons-nous?	Which way shall we go?
Allez par ici — par là,	Go this way — that way.
C'est le plus court,	It is the nighest way.
Par où il vous plaira,	Which way you please.
A la main gauche ou à droite,	On the left hand or to the right.
A main gauche ou à gauche,	On the left hand or to the left.
Restez là — venez ici,	Stay there — come here.
Traversons ici la rue,	Let us cross the street here.
Enfilons cette cour-ci,	Let us go through this court.
Vous marchez bien vite,	You walk too fast.
Je ne saurais vous suivre,	I cannot go so fast.
Vous allez trop vite,	You go too fast.
Vous êtes un mauvais marcheur, m.	You are a bad walker.
Allez un peu plus doucement,	Go a little slower.
Etes vous las, m. lasse, f.	Are you tired?
Je suis fort fatigué, m. e, f.	I am very much tired.
Reposons-nous un peu,	Let us rest a little.
Entrons dans ce café-ci,	Let us go into this coffee-house.

IV.

DES JOURS, DES MOIS, ET DES SAISONS.
Of the Days, Months, and Seasons.

J'irai à Londres Lundi ou Mardi prochain.	I shall go to London on Monday or Tuesday next.
Je reviendrai Mercredi.	I will return on Wednesday.
Mon frère partira Jeudi ou Vendredi.	My brother will set out Thursday or Friday.
Je lui écrirai Samedi ou Dimanche.	I will write to him on Saturday or Sunday.
Il fait froid aux mois de Janvier et de Février.	It is cold in the months of January and February.
Les jours sont longs au mois de Mars.	The days are long in the month of March.
La nature semble revivre au mois d'Avril.	Nature seems to revive in the month of April.

Les arbres sont en fleurs au mois de Mai.	The trees are in bloom in the month of May.
On fauche les prés au mois de Juin et de Juillet.	The meadows are mowed in the months of June and July.
On commence à couper les blés au mois d'Août.*	They begin to cut down the wheat in the month of August.
La moisson est presque finie au mois de Septembre.	The harvest is almost over in the month of September.
Les jours sont fort raccourcis au mois d'octobre.	The days are much shortened in the month of October.
Le feu commence à être de saison au mois de Novembre.	Fire begins to be comfortable in the month of November.
Il fait bientôt nuit à la fin de Décembre.	It soon grows dark at the end of December.
Le Printemps est agréable; l'Eté est ordinairement chaud ; l'Automne est tempéré, et l'Hiver est froid.	The Spring is pleasant ; the Summer is generally hot ; the Autumn is mild, and the Winter is cold.

V.

POUR MANGER ET POUR BOIRE.

For Eating and Drinking.

J'ai faim; j'ai grand'faim,	I am hungry; I am very hungry.
Donnez-moi quelque chose à manger,	Give me something to eat.
Que voulez-vous manger; du pain et du beurre ?	What will you eat; some bread and butter ?
Apportez-moi quelque autre chose,	Bring me something else.
Voulez-vous du rôti ou du bouilli ?	Will you have roast or boiled meat ?
Voici du mouton, du bœuf, du veau, et du lard,	Here is some mutton, beef, veal and bacon.
Nous avons aussi du jambon, qui est excellent,	We have also a ham which is very nice.
En souhaitez-vous manger ?	Do you choose to eat any ?
Voilà une assiette, un couteau et une fourchette,	There is a plate, a knife and a fork.
Du pain rassis et du pain frais,	Some stale and new bread.
Du fromage et des fruits,	Some cheese and fruit.
Servez vous, monsieur,	Help yourself, sir.
J'ai assez mangé,	I have eaten enough.
J'ai soif; j'ai grand'soif,	I am dry; I am very dry.
Donnez-moi à boire,	Give me some drink.
Votre petite bière n'est pas bonne,	Your small beer is not good.
Je la trouve trop amère,	I think it is too bitter.
Apportez-moi un verre d'eau et de vin,	Bring me a glass of wine and water.
A présent, j'ai mangé et bu suffisamment,	Now I have eaten and drunk quite sufficient.
Otez tout ceci,	Take away all these things.

VI.

CE QUI CONCERNE L'ÉCOLE ET LEE ÉCOLIERS.

Concerning the School and the Schoolars.

Où est votre livre ?	Vhere is your book ?
Voilà votre grammaire,	There is your grammar.
Asseyez-vous à votre place,	Sit down in your place.
Lisez votre leçon,	Read your lesson.
Vous lisez trop vite,	You read too fast.
Lisez plus doucement,	Read slower.
Etudiez votre leçon,	Study your lesson.
Apprenez-la tout bas,	Get it to yourself.
Vous ne faites que badiner,	You do nothing but play.
Je vous marquerai,	I will set you down.
Faites-moi un peu de place,	Make me a little room.
Vous avez assez de place,	You have room enough.
Reculez-vous un peu,	Sit a little farther.
Un peu plus haut,	A little higher.
Un peu plus bas,	A little lower.
Donnez moi mon livre,	Give me my book.
Où commençons-nous?	Where do we begin?
Jusqu'où disons-nous?	How far do we say?
Jusqu'ici, et pas plus loin,	So far and no farther.
A qui est ce livre?	Whose book is this?
Je ne sais pas à qui il est,	I don't know whom it belongs to.
Quelle est votre tâche?	Where is your task?
Savez-vous votre leçon?	Can you say your lesson?
Pas encore ; elle est longue et difficile. Soufflez-moi.	Not yet; it is very long and hard. Prompt me.
Vous êtes un bredouilleur.	You are a stammerer.
Prononcez plus distinctement,	Pronounce more distinotly.
Avez-vous une plume, de l'encre et du papier?	Have you got a pen, some ink and paper?
Ecrivez votre devoir,	Write your exercise.
Vous l'avez mal écrit,	You have done it badly.
Il est plein de fautes,	It is full of faults.
Allez le récrire,	Go and write it over again.
Et dépêchez-vous,	And make haste.
Dites *ou* récitez votre leçon,	Say *or* repeat your lesson.
Montrez-moi votre traduction,	Show me your translation.
Je ne l'ai pas encore faite,	I have not wrote it yet.
Vous serez puni *m.* punie *f.*	You shall be punished.
A quelle heure vous êtes-vous levé ce matin?	At what o'clock did you get up this morning?
A huit heures,	At eight o'clock
Pourquoi ne vous êtes-vous pas levé plus tôt?	Why did you not get up sooner?
Personne ne m'a éveillé *m.*	Nobody called me up.
Vous êtes un paresseux,	You are a sluggard.
Demeurez à votre place,	Keep in your place.
Otez-vous de ma place,	Get out of my place.

Pourquoi me poussez-vous comme cela?	Why do you push me *or* thrust me so?
Qui est-ce qui vous pousse?	Who pushes you?
Je me plaindrai de vous,	I'll complain of you.
Faites-le, si vous voulez,	Do it, if you will.
Je ne m'en soucie point,	I don't care for that.
Vous êtes un rapporteur,	You are a tell-tale.
Taisez-vous,	Hold your tongue.
Tenez-vous tranquille,	Be quiet, *or* be still.
Il a craché sur mes habits,	He has spit upon my clothes.
Il m'a donné un soufflet,	He gave me a box on the ear.
Il m'a égratigné le visage,	He scratched my face.
Il a déchiré mon livre,	He has torn my book.
C'est un espiègle,	He is a mischievous boy.
Vous êtes un vaurien,	You are a wicked boy.
Monsieur, il m'empêche d'apprendre ma leçon,	Sir, he hinders me from getting my lesson.
Il me pousse hors de ma place,	He thrusts me out of my place.
Il me donne des coups de pied,	He kicks me
Pourquoi l'avez-vous dénoncé au Maître?	Why did you tell the Master of him?
Je vous en ferai repentir,	I will make you repent of it.
Mêlez-vous de vos affaires,	Mind your own business.

FIN.

ELEMENTS OF FRENCH GRAMMAR

GRAMMATICAL RULES

PARTS OF SPEECH.

THERE are ten parts of speech, or sorts-of words; six of which, namely, the article, the substantive or noun substantive, the adjective or noun adjective, the pronoun, the verb and the participle, are variable, that is, are liable to vary in their termination; and the remaining four, namely, the adverb, the preposition, the conjunction and the interjection, are invariable, that is, never change.

The substantive serves to name a person or thing, as HENRI, Henry; BATON, stick.

The adjective is a word added to a substantive to express some quality or property of a person or a thing; as "AIMABLE enfant," amiable child; "rose BLANCHE," white rose.

The peculiar adjective-words UN, UNE, a or an; and LE, LA, LES, the, are called "articles."

The verb is a word by which we express that persons or things do any thing, or are any thing, or have any thing done to them; as "Charles LIT," Charles reads. "Le bœuf EST utile"—The ox is useful. "Un bon élève EST RÉCOMPENSÉ par son maître"—A good pupil is rewarded by his master.

The pronoun is a word that stands for a noun, to avoid repetition; as, "L'enfant est fatigué, IL dort"—The child is tired, he is asleep.

The participle is so called because it participates of both the adjective and the verb; as, "un chien DORMANT"—a sleeping dog; "un bâton ROMPU" a broken stick.

The adverb is a word added to a verb, an adjective, or another adverb, to express some circumstance, modifying such verb, adjective, or adverb; as, "servir FIDÈLEMENT"—to serve faithfully; "TRÈS-grand," very great; "FORT bien," very well.

The preposition serves to denote a relation between two words; as, "Je viens DE Paris"—I come from Paris.

The conjunction is used to connect words or sentences together; as, "Dieu ET mon droit"—God and and my right. "Soyons heureux, MAIS soyons sages"—Let us be happy, but let us be wise.

The interjection expresses a sudden emotion; as, HA! HÉLAS!

ARTICLE.

There are in French three articles, the definite, the indefinite, and the partitive. They agree in gender and number with the noun to which they relate.

DEFINITE ARTICLE

The definite article is LE, LA, LES, the.
3. LE is masculine singular; as, "le père," the father.
4. LA is féminine singular; as, "la mère," the mother.
5. L' (apostrophe, see page 1) is singular of either gender; as, "l'enfant" the child.
6. LES is plural of either gender; as, "les enfants," the children.

When LE or LES is preceded by DE, of *or* from, or by $\grave{a}$, to *or* at, DE LE is contracted into DU, DE LES into DES, $\grave{a}$ *le* into AU, and $\grave{a}$ *les* into AUX; therefore :—
7. DU is used instead of *de le*.
8. DES is used instead of *de les*.
9. AU is used instead of $\grave{a}$ *le*.
10. AUX is used instead of $\grave{a}$ *les*

INDEFINITE ARTICLE.

The indefinite article is UN, UNE, a or an.
11. UN is masculine singular; as, "un frère," a brother.
12. UNE is feminine singular; as, "une sœur," a sister.

PARTITIVE ARTICLE.

13. The partitive article is DU, DE LA, DE L' or DES, some *or* any.
14. *Some* or *any* is often understood in English, but in French the article DU, DE LA, DE L' or DES, is always used before a noun taken in a partitive sense, as :

Il a apporté du papier, de l'encre et   He has brought paper, ink
  des plumes.
Avez-vous de la cire ?—Non, mais   Have you any wax ?—N , but I have
  j'ai des pains à cacheter.   some wa

15. When a noun is preceded by an adjective, and is taken vaguely in a partitive sense, DE is used without the article, as :

Cet homme a de grands talents.   That man has great talents.

But the article is used whenever the substantive is taken in a particular sense, or is considered as forming, with the adjective, a compound word, as :

Voilà de la bonne viande.   There is some good meat,
Voici des petits pains tout chauds.   Here are some rolls quite hot.

16. ENGLISH CONSTRUCTIONS INVERTED BY TRANSLATION INTO FRENCH.

When the English possessive case is expressed by '*s*, as in "my father's house," the words are rendered in an inverted manner in French, and their relation is conveyed by the preposition DE, as :

My father's house.—"La maison de mon père," literally, the house of my father.
The child's toys.—"Les jouets de l'enfant;" literally, the toys of the child.
A mother's affection.—"L'affection d'une mère," literally, the affection of a mother.

The preposition DE is also put between the name of the thing and the name of the matter of which it is made, and this is in French always the last ; as,

>   A leather shoe.   Un soulier de cuir.
>   A paper hat.   Un chapeau de papier.
>   A silk handkerchief.   Un mouchoir de soie.
>   Thread stockings.   Des bas de fil.

SUBSTANTIVES.

FORMATION OF THE PLURAL OF SUBSTANTIVES.

GENERAL RULE

17. The plural of substantives is formed by adding an *s* to the singular; as, FEUILLE, leaf, FEUILLES, leaves.

EXCEPTIONS.

18. Substantives ending with *s*, *x*, or *z*, in the singular, do not vary the plural; as, BRAS, arm, BRAS, arms; NOIX, nut, NOIX, nuts; NEZ, nose, NEZ, noses.

19. Substantives ending with AU, EU, or OU, take an *x*; as, MARTEAU, hammer, MARTEAUX, hammers; FEU, fire, FEUX, fires; JOUJOU, toy, JOUJOUX, toys.

20. BLEU, blue, CLOU, nail, and a few more substantives in OU, follow the general rule; that is, take an *s* : BLEUS, CLOUS.

21. Substantives ending with *al*, or *ail*, change these terminations into AUX; as, CHEVAL, horse, CHEVAUX, horses; TRAVAIL, work, TRAVAUX, works.

22. BAL, ball, ÉVENTAIL, fan, and a few more substantives in *al*, *ail*, follow the general rule; that is, take *s* : BALS, ÉVENTAILS.

23. The following are irregular : ŒIL, eye, YEUX, eyes, (œils in some instances;) aïeul, grand-father, aïeuls, grand-fathers; aïeux, ancestors; CIEL, heaven, sky; CIEUX, heavens (CIELS in some instances.)

ADJECTIVES.

24. The adjective agrees in gender and number with the substantive to witch it relates : as, UN BEAU CHIEN, a fine dog ; UNE MAISON BLANCHE, a white house ; DEUX CHEVAUX NOIRS, two black horses.

25. If the adjective relates to several substantives, it is put in the plural; as,

Mon père et mon frère sont heureux.   My father and brother are happy.
Ma mère et ma sœur sont heureuses.   My mother and sister are happy.

26. If the substantives to which the adjective relates are of different genders, it is put in the masculine plural ; as,

Mon père et ma mère sont heureux.   My father and mother are happy.

FORMATION OF THE FEMININE OF ADJECTIVES.

27. An adjective is made feminine by the addition of an e mute to the masculine termination, as GRAND, GRANDE, great, large, tall; PETIT, PETITE, little, small.

28. Adjectives ending in the masculine with e mute do not change for the feminine; as UTILE, useful; SÉVÈRE, severe.

29. Adjectives ending with EL, EIL, IEN, ON, AS, or ET, double their last consonant and take e mute; as CRUEL, CRUELLE, cruel; PAREIL, PAREILLE, like, CHRÉTIEN, CHRÉTIENNE, christian; BON, BONNE, good; LAS, LASSE, tired; MUET, MUETTE, dumb.

30. RAS, shorn, makes in the feminine RASE. COMPLET, DISCRET, INQUIET, SECRET, make COMPLÈTE, DISCRÈTE, INQUIÈTE, SECRÈTE. CHER, dear, makes CHÈRE.

31. Adjectives ending witg f change f into ve; as NEUF, NEUVE, new.

32. Adjectives ending with x change x into se; as HEUREUX, HEUREUSE, happy; NOMBREUX, NOMBREUSE, numerous; JALOUX, JALOUSE, jealous.

33. Adjectives ending with EUR generally change EUR into EUSE; as TROMPEUR, TROMPEUSE, deceitful.

34. Antérieur, extérieur, inférieur, intérieur, majeur, mineur, meilleur, supérieur, *take* e *mute.* Accusateur, conducteur, créateur, protecteur, *make in the feminine,* accusatrice, conductrice, etc. Vengeur, enchanteur, *make* vengeresse, enchanteresse.

35. Among other adjectives which form their feminine irregularly are :

MAS.	FEM.		MAS.	FEM.	
Beau, Bel	belle,	fine, beautiful.	Mou, Mol,	molle,	soft.
Blanc.	blanche,	white.	Nouveau, Nouvel,	nouvelle,	new.
Doux,	douce,	sweet.	Nul (ne,)	nulle,	no.
Epais,	épaisse,	thick.	Public,	publique,	public.
Favori,	favorite,	favorite.	Roux,	rousse,	red.
Faux,	fausse,	false.	Sec,	sèche,	dry.
Fou, Fol	folle,	mad.	Sot,	sotte,	silly.
Frais,	fraîche,	fresh.	Tiers,	tierce,	third.
Franc,	franche,	frank.	Traître,	traîtresse,	traitor.
Gentil,	gentille,	pretty.	Turc,	turque,	turk.
Gros,	grosse,	big.	Vieux, Vieil	vieille,	old.
Long,	longue,	long.			
Malin,	maligne,	malignant.			

36. BEAU, FOU, MOU, NOUVEAU, VIEUX, are used before a consonant or *h* aspirated; but BEL, FOL, MOL, NOUVEL, VIEIL, are used before a vowel or silent *h*.

FORMATION OF THE PLURAL OF ADJECTIVES.

37. The plural of adjectives is generally formed like the plural of substantives. Many adjectives in AL form their plural in AUX, as ÉGAL, ÉGAUX, equal.

PLACE OF ADJECTIVES.

38. Adjectives in French are generally placed after substantives; as, UNE CHAMBRE CARRÉE, a square room; UNE NUIT OBSCURE, a dark night.

39. The following adjectives usually precede the substantives: BEAU, fine; BON, good; CHER, dear (denoting affection;) DIGNE, worthy; GRAND, great, JEUNE, young; JOLI, pretty; MAUVAIS, bad; MÉCHANT, wicked; MEILLEUR, better; MOINDRE, less; PETIT, little; VIEUX, old.

DEGREES OF COMPARISON.

There are three degrees of comparison:—1. The POSITIVE, or the adjective itself. 2. The COMPARATIVE, expressed by *plus*, more, or *moins*, less, placed before the adjective. 3. The SUPERLATIVE, expressed by LE, LA, or LES PLUS, the most; LE, LA, or LES MOINS, the last, placed before the adjective: as,

POSITIVE.	COMPARATIVE.	SUPERLATIVE.
Digne, worthy.	*plus digne*, worthier. *moins digne*, less worthy.	*le plus digne*, the worthiest. *le moins digne*, the least worthy.

40. To denote a comparaison of equality, AUSSI, as, is placed before the adjective, and QUE, as, after it; as, HENRI EST AUSSI ATTENTIF QUE ROBERT. Henry is as attentive as Robert.

41. To denote a comparison of superiority, PLUS, more, is placed before the adjective, and QUE, than, after it; as, CHARLES EST PLUS GRAND QUE LOUIS. Charles is taller than Lewis.

42. To denote a comparison of inferiority, MOINS, less, is placed before the adjective, and QUE, than, after it; as, CAROLINE EST MOINS INSTRUITE QUE LOUISE. Caroline is less learned than Louisa.

THE SUPERLATIVE DEGREE.

When the quality is expressed in a very high degree, without implying a comparison, the superlative is called absolute, and is formed with some adverb of degree, such as, TRÈS, FORT, BIEN, very; EXTRÊMEMENT, extremely; EXCESSIVEMENT, excessively, etc., before the adjective; as, MA MÈRE EST TRÈS-HEUREUSE. My mother is very happy.

44. When the superlative expresses a comparison with other objects, it is called relative, and is formed by prefixing LE, LA, LES, MON, MA, etc., to the adverbs PLUS and MOINS; as, LA PLUS APPLIQUÉE DE VOS SŒURS, the most sedulous of your sisters; LE PLUS HEUREUX DES HOMMES, the happiest of men.

45. The following adjectives form their degrees of comparison irregularly: BON, good; MEILLEUR, better; LE MEILLEUR, the best.

MAUVAIS, bad; PIRE or PLUS MAUVAIS, worse; LE PIRE or LE PLUS MAUVAIS the worst.
PETIT, little or small; MOINDRE, or PLUS PETIT, less or smaller; LE MOINDRE or LE PLUS PETIT, the last or smallest.

46. The comparative of these adjectives must not be mistaken for the comparative of their corresponding adverbs:
BIEN, well; MIEUX, better; LE MIEUX, the best.
MAL, badly; PIS or PLUS MAL, worse; LE PIS or LE PLUS MAL, the worst.
PEU, little; MOINS, less; LE MOINS, LEAST.

NUMERALS.

47. The cardinal numbers are:

Un, one.	Onze, eleven.
Deux, two.	Douze, Twelve.
Trois, three.	Treize, thirteen.
Quatre, four.	Quatorze, fourteen.
Cinq, five.	Quinze, fifteen.
Six, six.	Seize, sixteen.
Sept, seven.	Dix-sept, seventeen.
Huit, eight.	Dix-huit, eighteen.
Neuf, nine.	Dix-neuf, nineteen.
Dix, ten.	
Vingt, twenty.	Vingt-cinq, twenty five.
Vingt et un, twenty-one.	Vingt-six, twenty-six.
Vingt-deux, twenty-two.	Vingt-sept, twenty-seven.
Vingt-trois, twenty-three.	Vingt-huit, twenty-eight.
Vingt-quatre, twenty-four.	Vingt-neuf, twenty-nine.
Trente, thirty.	Trente-cinq, thirty-five.
Trente et un, thirty-one.	Trente-six, thirty-six.
Trente-deux, thirty-two.	Trente-sept, thirty-seven.
Trente-trois, thirty-three.	Trente-huit, thirty-eight.
Trente-quatre, thirty-four.	Trente-neuf, thirty-nine.
Quarante, forty.	Cinquante, fifty.
Quarante et un, forty-one.	Cinquante et un, fifty-one.
Soixante, sixty.	Soixante et dix, seventy.
Soixante et un, sixty-one.	Soixante et onze, seventy-one.
Quatre-vingt, eighty.	Quatre-vingt-dix, ninety.
Quatre-vingt-un, eighty-one.	Quatre-vingt-onze, ninety-one.
Cent, a hundred.	Mille, a thousand.

48. *Mille* is spelt *mil*, when it refers to the Christian era; as, *l'an mil huit cent cinquante-quatre*, the year 1854.

49. The ordinal numbers are:

Premier, first.	Neuvième, ninth.
Second, } second.	Dixième, tenth.
Deuxième, }	Onzième, eleventh.
Troisième, third.	Douzième, twelfth.
Quatrième, fourth.	Vingtième, twentieth.
Cinquième, fifth.	Vingt et unième, twenty-first.
Sixième, sixth.	Vingt-deuxième, twenty-second.
Septième, seventh.	Trentième, thirtieth.
Huitième, eighth.	Quarantième, etc., fortieth.

50. The distributive numbers (fractions) are:
La moitié, the half.
Le tiers, the third.
Le quart, the fourth.
Les trois quarts, the three fourths.
Le cinquième, the fifth.
Le sixième, the sixth.
Le septième, the seventh.
The rest like the ordinal numbers.

51. In speaking of sovereigns, or the days of the month, the cardinal numbers are generally used; as, LOUIS QUATORZE, ROI DE FRANCE. Louis the XIVth, king of France. LE DEUX AVRIL. The second of April.

52. Except in mentioning the first; as, HENRI 1ER. Henry the 1st. LE PREMIER JANVIER. The 1st of January.

PRONOUNS.

PERSONAL PRONOUNS.

53. The following pronouns are called conjunctive, because they are immediately united with verbs:

SUBJECT OR	OBJECTIVE CASES.	
NOMINATIVE CASE.	DATIVE.	ACCUSATIVE.
je, I.	me, to me.	me, me.
tu, thou.	te, to thee.	te, thee.
il, he, it, elle, she, it.	lui, { to him, to her, to it.	le, him, it. la, her, it.
nous, we.	nous, to us.	nous, us.
vous, you.	vous, to you.	vous, you.
ils, elles, } they.	leur, to them.	les, them

SE, himself, herself, itself, one's self, themselves, each, or one another, or to himself, to herself, to itself, to one's self, to themselves etc.
Y, to him, her, it, them, etc.
EN, of or from him, her, it, them, etc.

54. Conjunctive personnal pronouns in the accusative or dative are always placed before the verb; unless the verb be in the imperative affirmative (see Rule 59); as,

Je vous vois.   I see you.
Il me parle.   He speaks to me.
Prenez-le.   Take it.

55. In interrogations, the pronoun in the nominative case comes after the verb; as, PARLEZ-VOUS FRANÇAIS? Do you speak French?

56. The following pronouns are called disjunctive, because they are used independently of the verb, or separated from it:

SINGULAR.

NOMINATIVE AND ACCUSATIVE. }	MOI, I, me,	TOI, thou, thee,	LUI, he, him,	ELLE, she, her,	SOI, one's self.

PLURAL

NOMINATIVE AND ACCUSATIVE	NOUS, we, us	VOUS, you,	EUX, they, them.	ELLES, they, them.

57. The disjunctive personal pronouns are often connected with the word "même," self:

moi-même, myself.
toi-même, thyself.
lui-même, himself.
elle-même, herself.
soi-même, one's self.

nous-mêmes, ourselves.
vous-même, yourself.
vous-mêmes, yourselves
eux-mêmes, } themselves.
elles-mêmes, }

58. The disjunctive pronouns are found after a verb or a preposition, and sometimes are used alone for the sake of emphasis; as, "C'est moi." It is I. "Parle-t-il de moi?" Does he speak of me? "Lui, il est Allemand." He is a German.

58. Personal pronouns are placed after the verb in the imperative affirmative; as "Prenez-le." Take it. "Parlez-leur." Speak to them.

60. After the imperative affirmative, MOI and TOI are substituted for me and te, except when followed by EN; as, "Donnez-moi un livre." Give me a book.

POSSESSIVE PRONOUNS.

61. The following, being always used with nouns, are called pronouns adjective:

SINGULAR		PLURAL.	
MASC.	FEM.	OF BOTH GENDERS.	
mon,	ma,	mes,	my,
ton,	ta,	tes,	thy,
son,	sa,	ses,	his, her, its, one's,
notre,		nos,	our.
votre,		vos,	your.
leur,		leurs,	their.

62. The following, having a reference to nouns understood, are called disjunctive possessive pronouns:

le mien,	la mienne,	les miens,	les miennes,	mine.
le tien,	la tienne,	les tiens,	les tiennes,	thine.
le sien,	la sienne,	les siens,	les siennes,	{ his, her, its, one's own.
le nôtre,	la nôtre,		les nôtres,	ours.
le vôtre,	la vôtre,		les vôtres,	yours.
le leur,	la leur,		les leurs,	theirs.

63. Possessive pronouns agree in gender and number with the object possessed, and never, as in English, with the possessor; as, "son mari," her husband; "sa sœur," his or her sister.

64. MON, TON SON, are used instead of MA, TA, SA, before nouns feminine beginning with a vowel or h mute; as, "mon âme," my soul; "son épouse," his wife.

RELATIVE PRONOUNS

65. The relative pronouns are those which relate to a preceding noun or pronoun, which is called antecedent, and with which they agree in gender, number and person. They are :

"qui," who, which, that.
"de qui," of *or* from whom, whose; "dont," of *or* from whom, of *or* from which, whose; "de quoi," of *or* from what.
"à qui," to whom; "à quoi," to what.
"que," whom, which, that.
"lequel, m. s., laquelle, f. s., lesquels, m. pl., lesquelles, f. pl.," which, whom, that.

66. The following are interrogative :

"qui"? who *or* whom ? "qui est-ce qui? de qui"? etc.
"quoi? que? qu'est-ce que"? what? "de quoi"? etc.
"lequel? m. s., laquelle? f. s., lesquels? m. pl., lesquelles"? f. pl., which ?

67. The following are always used with a substantive :

"quel, m. s., quelle, f. s., quels, m. pl., quelles, f. pl.," what ? which ?

DEMONSTRATIVE PRONOUNS.

68. The demonstrative pronouns serve to point out the thing or things spoken of. The following are called pronouns adjective :

SINGULAR.		PLURAL.
MASC.	FEM.	OF BOTH GENDERS.
ce, cet,	cette, this, that.	ces, these, those.

69. *Cet* is used before a noun masculine beginning with a vowel or a silent *h*.

70. *Ce* is much used with *est*, is, and corresponds with the English *it ;* as, *C'est vous.* It is you. *C'est un livre.* It is a book.

71. *Ci,* here, and *là,* there, are sometimes added to the noun after, *ce, cette, ces ;* as, *ce livre-ci,* this book,; *cette plume-là,* that pen.

72. The following demonstrative pronouns refer to an object not named:

    ceci, this ; as, *Ceci est utile,* This is useful.
    cela, that ;   *Cela est inutile,* That is useless.

73. The following point out an object previously mentioned :

    celui, m. s., *celle,* f. s., this, that.
    ceux, m. pl., *celles,* f. pl., these, those.

| *celui-ci,* m. s. *celle-ci,* f. s. | this one. | *celui-là,* m. s. *celle-là,* f. s. | that one. |
| *ceux-ci,* m. pl. *celles-ci,* f. pl. | these | *ceux-là,* m. pl. *celles-là,* f. pl. | those |

74. *Ce, celui, ceux,* and *celles,* are also used with a relative pronoun in reference to a noun previously expressed ; as, *Celui qui fait son devoir—* He who does his duty. *Celui que j'aime—*He whom I love.

PRONOUNS AND ADJECTIVES INDEFINITE.

75. Pronouns and adjectives indefinite have a vague and general signification; as,

ON, L'ON, one, they, people.
PLUSIEURS, several.
AUTRE, other.
AUTRUI, other people, others.
CHACUN, each, every one.
PERSONNE, anybody.
PERSONNE (NE), nobody.
TEL, he, who, such, such a one.
QUELQU'UN, somebody.
AUCUN, any one.
CERTAIN, certain.
CHAQUE, each, every.
QUI QUE CE SOIT, whoever.
QUOI QUE CE SOIT, whatever.

QUICONQUE, whoever.
QUELCONQUE, whatever, any.
QUELQUE, } some, a few.
QUELQUES, }
QUELQUES-UNS, some
QUELQUE...QUE, however.
L'UN L'AUTRE, one another.
L'UN ET L'AUTRE, both.
L'UN OU L'AUTRE, either.
NI L'UN NI L'AUTRE, neither.
NUL, no one.
TOUT, every thing.
TOUT...QUE, however.

76. AUTRE, CERTAIN, CHAQUE, QUELQUE, QUELCONQUE, PLUSIEURS, TEL, TOUT, AUCUN, NUL, are used adjectively.

VERBS.

77. The verb *être*, to be, as it expresses existence, is called a verb substantive; all other verbs, as they contain an attribute or quality, are called verbs attributive. These are divided into verbs active or transitive; verbs passive; verbs neuter or intransitive; verbs reflective, and verbs unipersonal or impersonal.

MOODS AND TENSES.

78. A verb has five moods: 1. The infinitive, which denotes an action or state in an indefinite manner; as, *aimer*, to love. 2. The indicative, which affirms positively; as, *Je parle*—I speak. 3. The conditional, which affirms conditionally; as, *Je parlerais si, etc.*—I would speak, if etc. 4. The imperative, which implies command, request; as, *Parle*—Speak. 5. The subjunctive, which denotes an action or state in a manner dependent on a preceding verb, which implies doubt, fear, or desire, and to which it is connected by the conjunction *que*; as, *Je doute qu'il vienne*—I doubt whether he will come.

The tenses express the division of time. The simple tenses are expressed by a single word; as, *Je travaille*—I work. The compound are formed by the verbs *avoir*, to have, and *être*, to be, which are then called auxiliary; as, *J'ai travaillé*—I have worked.

79.—AVOIR.

INFINITIVE MOOD.
PRESENT.— Avoir, to have.
PAST.— Avoir eu, to have had.

PARTICIPLES.
PRESENT.— Ayant, having.
PAST.— Eu, had. Ayant eu, having had.
FUTURE.— Devant avoir, about to have.

INDICATIVE MOOD.

PRESENT.
J'ai, I have.
Tu as, thou hast.
Il a, he has.
Nous avons, we have.
Vous avez, you have.
Ils ont, they have.

80. IMPERFECT.
J'avais, I had.
Tu avais, thou hadst.
Il avait, he had.
Nous avions, we had.
Vous aviez, you had.
Ils avaient, they had.

81. PASTE DEFINITE.
J'eus, I had.
Tu eus, thou hadst.
Il eut, he had.
Nous eûmes, we had.
Vous eûtes, you had.
Ils eurent, they had.

FUTURE.
J'aurai, I shall have.
Tu auras, thou wilt have.
Il aura, he will have.
Nous aurons, we shall have.
Vous aurez, you will have.
Ils auront, they will have.

COMPOUND TENSES.

PAST INDIFINITE.
J'ai eu, I have had.

82. PLUPERFECT.
J'avais eu, I had had.

83. PAST ANTERIOR.
J'eus eu, I had had.

FUTURE ANTERIOR.
J'aurai eu, I shall have had.

CONDITIONAL MOOD.

PRESENT.
J'aurais, I should have.
Tu aurais, thou wouldst have.
Il aurait, he would have.
Nous aurions, we should have.
Vous auriez, you would have.
Ils auraient, they would have.

PAST.
J'aurais eu, I should have had.

IMPERATIVE MOOD.

Aie, have thou.
Qu'il ait, let him have.
Ayons, let us have.
Ayez, have ye.
Qu'ils aient, let them have.

SUBJUNCTIVE MOOD.

84. PRESENT or FUTURE.

Que j'aie, that I may have.
Que tu aies, that thou mayst have.
Qu'il ait, that he may have.
Que nous ayons, that we may have.
Que vous ayez, that you may have.
Qu'ils aient, that they may have.

85. PAST PERFECT.

Que j'aie eu, that I may have had.

86. PERFECT.

Que j'eusse, that I might have.
Que tu eusses, that thou mightest have.
Qu'il eût, that he might have.
Que nous eussions, that we might have.
Que vous eussiez, that you might have.
Qu'ils eussent, that they might have.

87. PL. PERFECT.

Que j'eusse eu, that I might have had.

INTERROGATION WITH VERBS.

88. To conjugate a verb interrogatively, the pronoun nominative is placed after the verb; as, AVEZ-VOUS DE L'ARGENT? have you any money?

89. If the nominative is a noun, it is placed at the head of the sentence, and IL, ELLE, ILS, or ELLES, after the verb, according to the preceding rule: as, VOS FRÈRES ONT-ILS DE L'ARGENT? have your brothers any money?

90. The interrogation can also be formed by EST-CE QUE (is it that); as, EST-CE QUE VOTRE FRÈRE A DE L'ARGENT? has your brother any money? EST-CE QU'IL A DE L'ARGENT? has he any money?

91. The letter -T-, between two hyphens, is placed after a verb ending with a vowel and followed by IL, ELLE, or ON, in interrogations; as, A-T-IL DES PLUMES? has he any pens?

92. — ÊTRE.

INFINITIVE MOOD.

PRESENT. — Etre, to be.
PAST. — Avoir été, to have been.

PARTICIPLES.

PRESENT. — Etant, being.
PAST. — Eté, been. Ayant été, having been.
FUTURE. — Devant être, about to be.

INDICATIVE MOOD.

PRESENT.

Je suis, I am.
Tu es, thou art.
Il est, he is.
Nous sommes, we are.
Vous êtes, you are.
Ils sont, they are.

93. IMPERFECT.

J'étais, I was.
Tu étais, thou wast.
Il était, he was.
Nous étions, we were.
Vous étiez, you were.
Ils étaient, they were.

95. PAST DEFINITE.

Je fus, I was.
Tu fus, thou wast.
Il fut, he was.
Nous fûmes, we were.
Vous fûtes, you were.
Ils furent, they were.

FUTURE.

Je serai, I shall be.
Tu seras, thou wilt be.
Il sera, he will be.
Nous serons, we shall be.
Vous serez, you will be.
Ils seront, they will be.

COMPOUND TENSES.

PAST INDEFINITE

J'ai été, I have been.

96. PAST ANTERIOR.

J'eus été, I had been.

94. PLUPERFECT.

J'avais été, I had been.

FUTURE ANTERIOR.

J'aurai été, I shall have been.

CONDITIONAL MOOD.

PRESENT.

Je serais, I should be.
Tu serais, thou wouldst be.
Il serait, he would be.

Nous serions, we should be.
Vous seriez, you would be.
Ils seraient, they would be.

PAST.

J'aurais été, I should have been.

IMPERATIVE MOOD.

Sois, be (thou)
Qu'il soit, let him be.

Soyons, let us be.
Soyez, be (ye).
Qu'ils soient, let them be.

SUBJUNCTIVE MOOD.

97. PRESENT OR FUTURE.

Que je sois, that I may be.
Que tu sois, that thou mayst be.
Qu'il soit, that he may be.

Que nous soyons, that we may be.
Que vous soyez, that you may be.
Q'ils soient, that they may be.

98. PERFECT.

Que j'aie été,   that I may be.

99. IMPERFECT.

Que je fusse,   that I might be.   Que nous fussions,   that we might be.
Que tu fusses,   that thou mightst be.   Que vous fussiez,   that you might be.
Qu'il fût,   that he might be.   Qu'ils fussent,   that they might be.

100. PLUPERFECT.

Que j'eusse été,   that I might have been.

NEGATION WITH VERBS.

101. A negation is generally expressed in French by two words:

ne... pas, } not.	ne... nullement, } in no manner.
ne... point,	ne... aucunement, } by no means,
ne... personne, nobody.	ne... nulle part, nowhere.
ne... rien, nothing.	ne... que, only, but nothing but.
ne... jamais, never.	ne... ni, neither, no more.
ne... nul, } no, none,	ne... plus, no longer, no more.
ne... aucun,	ne... guère, but little.
	ne... goutte, not a jot.

102. The negative *ne* always precedes the verb; the other words, explanatory of the negation, generally follow the verb, but most of them may also be placed at the beginning of the sentence: as,

Il n'est pas heureux.   he is not happy.
Il ne consentira jamais.   he will never consent.
Jamais il ne consentira.   never will he consent.

CONJUGATION OF VERBS.

French verbs are divided into four conjugations, distinguished by the termination of the infinitive mood:

The first conjugation ends in ER,   as donner, to give.
　second..................IR,   finir, to finish.
　third....................OIR,   recevoir, to receive.
　fourth..................RE,   vendre, to sell.

The first conjugation has one model verb, the second has four, the third one, and the fourth four. A verb is said to be regular, when it is conjugated like one of those ten verbs.

103. MODEL VERB OF THE FIRST CONJUGATION.

(The first conjugation includes about 5,000 verbs conjugated like donner.)

INFINITIVE MOOD.

PRÉSENT.—Donner,   to give.
PAST.—Avoir donné,   to have given.

PARTICIPLES.

PRÉSENT.—Donnant, giving.
PAST.—Donné, given. Ayant donné, having given.
Future.—Devant donner, about to give.

INDICATIVE.

PRESENT.

Je donne, I give.
Tu donnes, thou givest.
Il donne, he gives.

Nous donnions, we give.
Vous donnez, you give.
Ils donnent, they give.

104. IMPERFECT.

Je donnais, I was giving.
Tu donnais, thou wast giving.
Il donnait, he was giving.

Nous donnons, we were giving.
Vous donniez, you were giving.
Ils donnaient, they were giving.

COMPOUND TENSES.

PAST INDEFINITE.   105. PLUSPERFECT.

J'ai donné, I have given.   J'avais donné, I have given.

*106. The simple tenses are formed in French with one word only. JE DONNE, is either I give, I do give, or I am giving. JE DONNAIS, I was giving or I used to give.

107. PAST DEFINITE.

Je donnai, I gave.
Tu donnas, thou gavest.
Il donna, he gave.

Nous donnâmes, we gave.
Vous donnâtes, you gave.
Ils donnèrent, they gave.

FUTURE.

Je donnerai, I shall give.
Tu donneras, thou wilt give.
Il donnera, he will give.

Nous donnerons, we shall give.
Vous donnerez, you will give.
Ils donneront, they will give.

PAST ANTERIOR.   FUTURE ANTERIOR.

J'eus donné, I had given.   J'aurai donné, I shall have given.

CONDITIONAL.

PRESENT.

Je donnerais, I should give.
Tu donnerais, thou wouldst give.
Il donnerait, he would give.

Nous donnerions, we should give.
Vous donneriez, you would give.
Ils donneraient, they would give.

PAST.

J'aurais donné, I should have given.
Tu aurais donné, thou wouldst have given.
Il aurait donné, he would have given.

Nous aurions donné, we should have given.
Vous auriez donné, you would have given.
Ils auraient donné, they would have given.

IMPERATIVE.

Donne, give (thou).
Qu'il donne, let him give.

Donnons, let us give.
Donnez, give (ye).
Qu'ils donnent, let them give.

SUBJUNCTIVE.

PRESENT OR FUTURE.

Que je donn e, that I may give.
Que tu donn es, that thou mayst give.
Qu'il donn e, that he may give.

Que nous donn ions, that we may give
Que vous donn iez, that you may give
Qu'ils donn ent, that they may give.

IMPERFECT

Que je donn asse, that I might give.
Que tu donn asses, that thou mighst give.
Qu'il donn ât, that he might give.

Que nous donn assions, that we might give.
Que vous donn assiez, that you might give.
Qu'ils donn assent, that they might give.

PERFECT.

Que j'aie donn é, that I may have given.

PLUPERFECT.

Que j'eusse donn é, that I might have given.

ORTHOGRAPHICAL REMARKS.

108. In verbs ending in GER, the E is retained after G before A, O, to preserve the articulation of G soft; as, CHANGER, to change; NOUS CHANGEONS, we change.

109. When C is pronounced like S, in the infinitive, it takes a CEDILLA before A, O, or U, to preserve its articulation; as, COMMENCER, to begin; COMMENÇANT, beginning.

110. Verbs which have Y before the termination of the infinitive or participle present, generally change it into I before E, ES, and ENT; as, EMPLOYER, to employ; J'EMPLOIE, I employ.

111. Verbs which have É (with an acute accent) or E mute in the infinitive or participle present require a grave accent on it (È) before a consonant followed by an E mute; as, ESPÉRER, to hope; il ESPÈRE, he hopes; MENER, to lead; IL MÈNE; he leads.

112. Verbs having E mute before the termination of the infinitive LER and TER, generally double L and T, when followed by E, ES, and ENT; as, APPELER, to call; JETER, to throw; J'APPELLE, I call; JE JETTE, I throw. Some take the grave accent on the E; ACHETER, to buy; IL ACHÈTE, he buys.

MODEL VERBS OF THE SECOND CONJUGATION.

The second conjugation is divided into four classes. Their model verbs are:

1. FINIR, to finish. 2. SERVIR, to serve. 3. OUVRIR, to open.
4. TENIR, to hold.

The first class consists of about 300 verbs.

The second consists of the verbs SERVIR, to serve; SENTIR, to feel; SORTIR, to go out; MENTIR, to lie; DORMIR, to sleep; PARTIR, to set out; SE REPENTIR, to repent; and their derivatives, such as DESSERVIR, etc.

The third consists of the verbs OUVRIR, to open; COUVRIR, to cover; OFFRIR, to offer; SOUFFRIR, to suffer; and their derivatives.

The fourth consists of the verbs TENIR, to hold; VENIR, to come; and their derivatives.

---

113. — FINIR.

INFINITIVE.

PRESENT.—Fin ir, to finish. PAST.—Avoir fin i, to have finished.

PARTICIPLES.

PRESENT.—Fin issant, finishing.
PAST.—Fin i, finished. Ayant fin i, having finished.
FUTURE.—Devant fin ir, about to finish.

INDICATIVE.

PRESENT.
I finish.
Je fin is.   Nous fin issons.
Tu fin is.   Vous fin issez.
Il fin it.   Ils fin issent.

PAST DEFINITE.
I finished.
Je fin is.   Nous fin îmes.
Tu fin is.   Vous fin îtes.
Il fin it.   Ils fin irent.

IMPERFECT.
I was finishing.
Je fin issais.   Nous fin issions.
Tu fin issais.   Vous fin issiez.
Il fin issait.   Ils fin issaient.

FUTURE.
I shall finish.
Je fin irai.   Nous fin irons.
Tu fin iras.   Vous fin irez.
Il fin ira.   Ils fin iront.

PAST INDEFINITE.
I have finished,
J'ai fin i, etc.

PAST ANTERIOR.
I had finished.
J'eus fin i, etc.

PLUPERFECT.
I had finished
J'avais fin i, etc.

FUTURE ANTERIOR.
I shall have finished.
J'aurai fin i, etc.

CONDITIONAL.		SUBJUNCTIVE.	
PRESENT.		**PRESENT OR FUTURE.**	
I should finish		*That I may finish.*	
Je fin irais.	Nous fin irions.	Que je fin isse.	Que nous fin issions.
Tu fin irais.	Vous fin iriez.	Que tu fin isses.	Que vous fin issiez.
Il fin irait.	Ils fin iraient.	Qu'il fin isse.	Qu'ils fin issent.
IMPERATIVE.		**IMPERFECT.**	
Finish (thou),		*That I might finish.*	
	Fin issons.	Que je fin isse.	Que nous fin issions.
Fin is.	Fin issez.	Que tu fin isses.	Que vous fin issiez
Qu'il fin isse.	Qu'ils fin issent.	Qu'il fin ît.	Qu'ils fin issent.

PAST COND.	PAST SUBJ.	PLUPERFECT SUBJ.
I shoud have finished.	*That I may have finished.*	*That I might have finished.*
J'aurais fin i, etc.	Que j'aie fin i, etc.	Que j'eusse fini, etc.

114. — SERVIR.

INFINITIVE.

PRESENT. — Serv ir, *to serve.*   PAST. — Avoir serv i, *to have served.*

PARTICIPLES.

PRESENT. — Serv ant, *Serving.*
PAST. — Serv i, *served.*   Ayant serv i, *having served.*
FUTURE. — Devant serv ir, *about to serve.*

INDICATIVE.

PRESENT.		PAST DEFINITE.	
I serve.		*I served.*	
Je ser s.	Nous serv ons.	Je serv is.	Nous serv îmes.
Tu ser s.	Vous serv ez.	Tu serv is.	Vous serv îtes.
Il ser t.	Ils serv ent.	Il serv it.	Ils serv irent.
IMPERFECT.		**FUTURE.**	
I was serving.		*I shall serve.*	
Je serv ais.	Nous serv ions.	Je serv irai.	Nous serv irons.
Tu serv ais.	Vous serv iez.	Tu serv iras.	Vous serv irez.
Il serv ait.	Ils serv aient.	Il serv ira.	Ils serv iront.
PAST INDEFINITE.		**PAST ANTERIOR.**	
I have served.		*I had served.*	
J'ai serv i.		J'eus serv i, etc.	

PLUPERFECT.
I had served.
J'avais serv i, etc.

FUTURE ANTERIOR.
I shall have served.
J'aurai serv i, etc.

CONDITIONAL.

PRESENT.
I should serve.
Je serv irais.   Nous serv irions.
Tu serv irais.   Vous serv iriez.
Il serv irait.   Ils serv iraient.

SUBJONCTIVE.

PRESENT OR FUTURE.
That I may serve.
Que je serv e.   Que nous serv ions.
Que tu serv es.   Que vous serv iez.
Qu'il serv e.   Qu'ils serv ent.

PAST.
I should have served.
J'aurais serv i, etc.

IMPERFCT.
That I might serve.
Que je serv isse.   Que nous serv issions.
Que tu serv isses. Que vous serv issiez.
Qu'il serv ît.   Qu'ils serv issent.

IMPERATIVE.
Serve (thou).
                    Serv ons.
Ser s*.   Serv ez.
Qu'il serv e.   Qu'il serv ent.

SUBJUNCTIVE.

PAST.
That I may have served,
Que j'aie serv i, etc.

PLUPERFECT.
That I might have served.
Que j'eusse serv i, etc.

* The *v* of the verbal root *serv* is thrown away in the singular of the indicative and imperative. The same with *t* and *m* of *sentir*, *sortir*, *dormir*, *partir*, *se repentir*, and their derivatives.

115. — OUVRIR.

INFINITIVE.

PRESENT. — Ouvr ir,   to open.
PAST. — Avoir ouv ert,   to have opened.

PARTICIPLES.

PRESENT. — Ouvr ant,   opening.
PAST. — Ouv ert,   opened.   Ayant ouv ert,   having opened.
FUTURE. — Devant ouvr ir,   about to open.

INDICATIVE.

PRESENT.		PAST DEFINITE.	
I open.		*I opened.*	
J'ouvr e.	Nous ouvr ons.	J'ouvr is.	Nous ouvr îmes.
Tu ouvr es.	Vous ouvr ez.	Tu ouvr is.	Vous ouvr îtes.
Il ouvr e.	Ils ouvr ent.	Il ouvr it,	Ils ouvr iront.

IMPERFECT.		FUTURE.	
I was opening.		*I shall open.*	
J'ouvr ais.	Nous ouvr ions.	J'ouvr irai.	Nous ouvr irons.
Tu ouvr ais.	Vous ouvr iez.	Tu ouvr iras.	Vous ouvr irez,
Il ouvr ait.	Ils ouvr aient.	Il ouvr ira.	Ils ouvr iront.

PAST INDEFINITE.	PAST ANTERIOR.
I have opened.	*I had opened.*
J'ai ouv ert, etc.	J'eus ouv ert, etc.

PLUPERFECT.	FUTURE ANTERIOR.
I had opened.	*I shall have opened.*
J'avais ouv ert, etc.	J'aurai ouv ert, etc.

CONDITIONAL.

PRESENT.
I should open.

		SUBJUNCTIVE.	
		PRESENT OR FUTURE.	
		That I may open.	
J'ouvr irais.	Nous ouvr irions,	Que j'ouvr e.	Que nous ouvr ions,
Tu ouvr irais.	Vous ouvr iriez,	Que tu ouvr es.	Que vous ouvr iez.
Il ouvr irait.	Ils ouvr iraient.	Qu'il ouvr e.	Qu'ils ouvr ent.

IMPERFECT.
That I might open.

PAST.	Que j'ouvr isse.	Que nous ouvr issions.
I should have opened.	Que tu ouvr isses.	Que vous ouvr issiez.
J'aurais ouv ert, etc.	Qu'il ouvr ît.	Qu'ils ouvr issent.

IMPERATIVE.			
Open (thou.)		PAST.	PLUPERFECT.
Ouvr e.	Ouvr ons.	*That I may have*	*That I might have*
Qu'il ouvr e.	Ouvr ez.	*opened.*	*opened.*
Qu'ils ouvr ent,		Que j'aie ouv ert, etc.	Que j'eusse ouv ert, etc.

116.—TENIR.

INFINITIVE.

PRESENT.—Ten ir, to hold.   PAST.—Avoir ten u, to have held.

PARTICIPLES

PRESENT.—Ten ant, holding.
PAST.—Ten u, held.   Ayant ten u, having held.
FUTURE.—Devant ten ir, about to hold.

INDICATIVE.

PRESENT.
I hold.

Je t iens.	Nous ten ons.	Je t ins.	Nous t înmes.
Tu t iens.	Vous ten ez.	Tu t ins.	Vous t întes.
Il t ient.	Ils t iennent.	Il t int.	Ils t inrent.

PAST DEFINITE.
I held.

IMPERFECT.
I was holding

Je ten ais.	Nous ten ions.	Je tiend rai.	Nous tiend rons.
Tu ten ais.	Vous ten iez.	Tu tiend ras.	Vous tiend rez.
Il ten ait.	Ils ten aient.	Il tiend ra.	Ils tiend ront.

FUTURE.
I shall hold.

PAST INDEFINITE.
I have held.
J'ai ten u, etc.

PAST ANTERIOR.
I had held.
J'eus ten u, etc.

PLUPERFECT.
I had held.
J'avais ten u, etc.

FUTURE ANTERIOR.
I shall have held.
J'aurai ten u, etc.

CONDITIONAL.

PRESENT.
I should hold.

Je tiend rais.	Nous tiend rions.	Que je t ienne.	Que nous ten ions.
Tu tiend rais.	Vous tiend riez.	Que tu t iennes.	Que vous ten iez.
Il tiend rait	Ils tiend raient.	Qu'il t ienne.	Qu'ils t iennent.

SUBJUNCTIVE.

PRESENT OR FUTURE.
That I may hold.

PAST.
I should have held.
J'aurais ten u, etc.

IMPERFECT.
That I might hold.

Que je t insse.	Que nous t inssions.
Que tu t insses.	Que vous t inssiez.
Qu'il t int.	Qu'ils t inssent.

IMPERATIVE.

Hold (thou).

T iens.
Qu'il t ienne.
Ten ons.
Ten ez.
Qu'ils t iennent.

PAST.
That I may have held.
Que j'aie ten u, etc.

PLUPERFECT.
That I might have held.
Que j'eusse ten u, etc.

MODEL VERB OF THE THIRD CONJUGATION.

The third conjugation consists of the verbs RECEVOIR, to receive, PERCEVOIR, to collect (rents, taxes, income); APERCEVOIR, to perceive; DEVOIR, to owe; REDEVOIR, to owe still; CONCEVOIR, to conceive; DÉCEVOIR, to deceive.

117.—RECEVOIR.

INFINITIVE MOOD.

PRESENT.—Rec evoir, to receive.
PAST.—Avoir reç u, to have received.

PARTICIPLES.

PRESENT.—Rec evant, receiving.
PAST.— Reç u, received. Ayant reç u, having received.
FUTURE.—Devant rec evoir, about to receive.

INDICATIVE.

PRESENT.
I receive.

Je reç ois   Nous rec evons
Tu reç ois   Vous rec evez
Il reç oit   Ils reç oivent

PAST DEFINITE.
I received.

Je reç us   Nous reç ûmes
Tu reç us   Vous reç ûtes
Il reç ut   Ils reç urent

IMPERFECT.
I was receiving.

Je rec evais   Nous rec evions
Tu rec evais   Vous rec eviez
Il rec evait   Ils rec evaient

FUTURE.
I shall receive.

Je rec evrai   Nous rec evrons
Tu rec evras   Vous rec evrez
Il rec evra   Ils rec evront

PAST INDEFINITE.
I have received.
J'ai reç u, etc.

PAST ANTERIOR.
I had received.
J'eus reç u, etc.

PLUPERFECT.
I had received.
J'avais reç u, etc.

FUTURE ANTERIOR.
I shall have received.
J'aurai reç u, etc.

CONDITIONAL.
PRESENT.
I should receive.

Je rec evrais.   Nous rec evrions.
Tu rec evrais.   Vous rec evriez.
Il rec evrait.   Ils rec evraient.

SUBJUNCTIVE.
PRESENT OR FUTURE.
That I may receive.

Que je reç oive.   Que nous rec evions.
Que tu reç oives.   Que vous rec eviez.
Qu'il reç oive.   Qu'ils reç oivent.

PAST.	IMPERFECT.
I should have received.	*That I might receive.*
J'aurais, reçu, etc.	Que je reç usse. Que nous reç ussions.
	Que tu reç usses. Que vous reç ussiez.
	Qu'il reç ût. Qu'ils reç ussent.

IMPERATIVE.	
Receive (thou).	PAST.
Reç ois.	*That I may have received.*
Qu'il reç oive.	Que j'aie reç u, etc.
Rec evons.	PLUPERFECT.
Rec evez.	*That I might have received.*
Qu'ils reç oivent.	Que j'eusse reç u, etc.

MODEL VERBS OF THE FOURTH CONJUGATION.

The fourth conjugation is divided into four classes :

The first ends in NDRE, RDRE (not preceded by I), as VENDRE, to sell ; PERDRE, to lose.

The second ends in AÎTRE, OÎTRE, as PARAÎTRE, to appear ; CROÎTRE, to grow.

The third ends in UIRE, as RÉDUIRE, to reduce.

The fourth ends in INDRE, as PLAINDRE, to pity.

119.—VENDRE.

INFINITIVE MOOD.

PRESENT.—Vend re, to sell.   PAST.—Avoir vend u, to have sold.

PARTICIPLES.

PRESENT. — Vend ant, selling.
PAST. — Vend u, sold. Ayant vend u, having sold.
FUTURE. — Devant vend re, about to sell.

INDICATIVE MOOD.

PRESENT.		PAST DEFINITE.	
I sell.		*I sold.*	
Je vend s.	Nous vend ons.	Je vend is.	Nous vend îmes.
Tu vend s.	Vous vend ez.	Tu vend is.	Vous vend îtes.
Il vend.	Ils vend ent.	Il vend it.	Ils vend irent.
IMPERFECT.		FUTURE.	
I was selling.		*I shall sell.*	
Je vend ais.	Nous vend ions.	Je vend rai.	Nous vend rons.
Tu vend ais.	Vous vend iez.	Tu vend ras.	Vous vend rez.
Il vend ait.	Ils vend aient.	Il vend ra.	Ils vend ront.

PAST INDEFINITE.
I have sold.
J'ai vend u, etc.

PAST ANTERIOR.
I had sold.
J'eus vend u, etc.

PLUPERFECT.
I had sold.
J'avais vend u, etc.

FUTURE ANTERIOR.
I shall have sold.
J'aurai vend u, etc.

CONDITIONAL.
PRESENT.
I should sell.

Je vend rais.	Nous vend rions.
Tu vend rais.	Vous vend riez.
Il vend rait.	Ils vend raient.

SUBJUNCTIVE.
PRESENT OR FUTURE.
That I may sell.

Que je vend e.	Que nous vend ions.
Que tu vend es.	Que vous vend iez.
Qu'il vend e.	Qu'ils vend ent.

PAST.
I should have sold.
J'aurais vend u, etc.

IMPERFECT.
That I might sell.

Que je vend isse.	Que nous vend issions.
Que tu vend isses.	Que vous vend issiez.
Qu'il vend ît.	Qu'ils vend issent.

IMPERATIVE.
Sell (thou).
Vend s.
Qu'il vend e.
Vend ons.
Vend ez.
Qu'ils vend ent.

PAST.
That I may have sold.
Que j'aie vend u, etc.

PLUPERFECT.
That I might have sold.
Que j'eusse vend u, etc.

119. — PARAÎTRE.

INFINITIVE MOOD.

PRESENT. — Par aître, to appear.
PAST. — Avoir par u, to have appeared.

PARTICIPLES.

PRESENT. — Par aissant, appearing.
PAST. — Par u, appeared. Ayant par u, having appeared.
FUTURE. — Devant par aître, about to appear.

INDICATIVE MOOD.

PRESENT.
I appear.

Je par ais.	Nous par aissons.
Tu par ais.	Vous par aissez.
Il par aît.	Ils par aissent.

PAST DEFINITE.
I appeared.

Je par us.	Nous par ûmes.
Tu par us.	Vous par ûtes.
Il par ut.	Ils par urent.

IMPERFECT.
I was appearing.

Je par aissais.	Nous par aissions.
Tu par aissais.	Vous par aissiez.
Il par aissait.	Ils par aissaient.

FUTURE.
I shall appear.

Je par aîtrai.	Nous par aîtrons.
Tu par aîtras.	Vous par aîtrez.
Il par aîtra.	Ils par aîtront.

PAST INDEFINITE.
I have appeared.
J'ai par u, etc.

PLUPERFECT.
I had appeared.
J'avais par u, etc.

PAST ANTERIOR.
I had appeared.
J'eus par u, etc.

FUTURE ANTERIOR.
I shall have appeared.
J'aurai par u, etc.

CONDITIONAL.

PRESENT.
I should appear.

Je par aîtrais.	Nous par aîtrions.
Tu par aîtrais.	Vous par aîtriez.
Il par aîtrait.	Ils par aîtraient.

SUBJUNCTIVE.

PRESENT OR FUTURE.
That I may appear.

Que je par aisse.	Que nous par aissions.
Que tu par aisses.	Que vous par aissiez.
Qu'il par aisse.	Qu'ils par aissent.

PAST.
I should have appeared.
J'aurais par u, etc,

IMPERFECT.
That I might appear.

Que je par usse.	Que nous par ussions.
Que tu par usses.	Que vous par ussiez.
Qu'il par ût.	Qu'ils par ussent.

IMPERATIVE.

Appear (thou).

Par ais.
Qu'il par aisse.
Par aissons.
Par aissez.
Qu'ils par aissent.

PAST.
That I may have appeared.
Que j'aie par u, etc.

PLUPERFECT.
That I might have appeared.
Que j'eusse par u, etc.

---

120. — RÉDUIRE.
INFINITIVE.
PRESENT. — Rédui re, to reduce.
PAST. — Avoir rédui t, to have reduced.

PARTICIPLES.

Present. — Rédui sant, reducing.
Past. — Rédui t, reduced. Ayant rédui t, having reduced.
Future. — Devant rédui re, about to reduce.

INDICATIVE.

PRESENT.
I reduce.

Je rédui s.   Nous rédui sons.
Tu rédui s.   Vous rédui sez.
Il rédui t.   Ils rédui sent.

IMPERFECT.
I was reducing.

Je rédui sais.   Nous rédui sions.
Tu rédui sais.   Vous rédui siez.
Il rédui sait.   Ils rédui saient.

PAST INDEFINITE.
I have reduced.
J'ai rédui t, etc.

PLUPERFECT.
I had reduced.
J'avais rédui t, etc.

PAST DEFINITE.
I reduced.

Je rédui sis.   Nous rédui sîmes.
Tu rédui sis.   Vous rédui sîtes.
Il rédui sit.   Ils rédui sirent.

FUTURE.
I shall reduce.

Je rédui rai.   Nous rédui rons.
Tu rédui ras.   Vous rédui rez.
Il rédui ra.   Ils rédui ront.

PAST ANTERIOR.
I had reduced.
J'eus rédui t, etc.

FUTURE ANTERIOR.
I shall have reduced.
J'aurai rédui t, etc.

CONDITIONAL.

PRESENT.
I should reduce.

Je rédui rais.   Nous rédui rions.
Tu rédui rais.   Vous rédui riez.
Il rédui rait.   Ils rédui raient.

PAST.
I should have reduced.
J'aurais rédui t, etc.

IMPERATIVE.

Reduce (thou).

Rédui s.
Qu'il rédui se.
Rédui sons.
Rédui sez.
Qu'ils rédui sent.

SUBJUNCTIVE.

PRESENT OR FUTURE.
That I may reduce.

Que je rédui se.   Que nous rédui-
　　　　　　　　　　sions.
Que tu rédui ses.   Que vous rédui-
　　　　　　　　　　siez.
Qu'il rédui se.   Qu'ils rédui sent.

IMPERFECT.
That I might reduce.

Que je rédui-   Que nous rédui-
　sisse.   　sissions.
Que tu rédui-   Que vous rédui-
　sisses.   　sissiez.
Qu'il rédui sît   Qu'ils rédui sissent.

PAST.
That I may have reduced.
Que j'aie rédui t, etc,

PLUPERFECT.
That I might have reduced.
Que j'eusse rédui t, etc.

121. — PLAINDRE.

INFINITIVE.

PRESENT. — Plaindre, to pity.
PAST. — Avoir plaint, to have pitied.

PARTICIPLES.

PRESENT. — Plaignant, pitying.
PAST. — Plaint, pitied. Ayant plaint, having pitied.
FUTURE. — Devant plaindre, about to pity.

INDICATIVE.

PRESENT.
I pity.
Je plains. Nous plaignons.
Tu plains. Vous plaignez.
Il plaint. Ils plaignent.

PAST DEFINITE.
I pitied.
Je plaignis. Nous plaignîmes.
Tu plaignis. Vous plaignîtes.
Il plaignit. Ils plaignirent.

IMPERFECT.
I was pitying.
Je plaignais. Nous plaignions.
Tu plaignais. Vous plaigniez.
Il plaignait. Ils plaignaient.

FUTURE.
I shall pity.
Je plaindrai. Nous plaindrons.
Tu plaindras. Vous plaindrez.
Il plaindra. Ils plaindront.

PAST INDEFINITE.
I have pitied.
J'ai plaint, etc.

PAST ANTERIOR.
I had pitied.
J'eus plaint, etc.

PLUPERFECT.
I had pitied.
J'avais plaint.

FUTURE ANTERIOR.
I shall have pitied.
J'aurai plaint, etc.

CONDITIONAL.

PRESENT.
I should pity.
Je plaindrais. Nous plaindrions.
Tu plaindrais. Vous plaindriez.
Il plaindrait. Ils plaindraient.

PAST.
I should have pitied.
J'aurais plaint, etc.

SUBJUNCTIVE.

PRESENT OR FUTURE.
That I may pity.
Que je plaigne. Que nous plaignions.
Que tu plaignes. Que vous plaigniez.
Qu'il plaigne. Qu'ils plaignent.

IMPERFECT.
That I might pity.
Que je plaignisse. Que nous plaignissions.
Que tu plaignisses. Que vous plaignissiez.
Qu'il plaignit. Qu'ils plaignissent.

IMPERATIVE.

Pity (thou).

Plai ns.
Qu'il plai gne.
Plai gnons.
Plai gnez.
Qu'ils plai gnent.

PAST.
That I may have pitied.
Que j'aie plai nt.

PLUPERFECT.
That I might have pitied
Que j'eusse plai nt.

PASSIVE VERBS.

122. A verb passive consists of the verb ETRE, and the PARTICIPLE PAST of a transitive verb. The participle agrees in gender and number with the nominative case, that is to say, the subject to which it relates; as,

Je suis aimé OR aimée. I am loved.
Tu es aimé OR aimée. Thou art loved.
Il est aimé. He is loved.
Elle est aimée. She is loved.
Nous sommes aimés OR aimées, etc.

NEUTER OR INTRANSITIVE VERBS.

123. The neuter or intransitive verbs are conjugated in their compound tenses with the auxiliary AVOIR, except the following, which are conjugated with ETRE:

Aller, to go.
Arriver, to arrive.
Décéder, to die.
Éclore, to blow, to hatch.
Intervenir, to intervene.
Mourir, to die.
Naître, to be born.
Parvenir, to attain.
Revenir, to come again.
Venir, to come.

Some neuter verbs are conjugated with both AVOIR and ETRE. With AVOIR they express an action, with ETRE the state resulting from that action; as,

Il a descendu au vestibule. He went down to the hall.
Maintenant, il est descendu. Now he is downstairs.

REFLECTIVE VERBS.

They are conjugated with two pronouns, and their compound tenses are formed by means of the auxiliary ETRE; as,

Je me suis habillé OR habillée. I have dressed myself.
Tu t'es habillé OR habillée. Thou hast dressed thyself.
Il s'est habillé. He has dressed himself.
Elle s'est habillée. She has dressed herself.
Nous nous sommes habillés OR ha- We have dressed ourselves, etc.

124—CONJUGATION OF A REFLECTIVE VERB.

INFINITIVE.

PRESENT.—Se lever (=to raise one's self up), to rise.
PAST.—S'être levé, to have risen.

PARTICIPLES.

PRESENT. — Se levant, rising.
PAST. — Levé, risen. S'étant levé, having risen.
FUTURE. — Devant se lever, about to rise.

INDICATIVE.

PRESENT.	IMPERFECT.
I rise.	*I was rising.*
Je me lève.	Je me levais.
Tu te lèves.	Tu te levais.
Il se lève.	Il se levait.
Nous nous levons.	Nous nous levions.
Vous vous levez.	Vous vous leviez.
Ils se lèvent.	Ils se levaient.

PAST DEFINITE.	FUTURE.
I rose.	*I shall rise.*
Je me levai.	Je me lèverai.
Tu te levas.	Tu te lèveras.
Il se leva.	Il se lèvera.
Nous nous levâmes.	Nous nous lèverons.
Vous vous levâtes.	Vous vous lèverez.
Ils se levèrent.	Ils se lèveront.

PAST INDEFINITE.	PLUPERFECT.
I have risen.	*I had risen.*
Je me suis levé.	Je m'étais levé.
Tu t'es levé.	Tu t'étais levé.
Il s'est levé.	Il s'était levé.
Nous nous sommes levés.	Nous nous étions levés.
Vous vous êtes levés.	Vous vous étiez levés.
Ils se sont levés.	Ils s'étaient levés.

PAST ANTERIOR.	FUTURE ANTERIOR.
I had risen.	*I shall have risen.*
Je me fus levé.	Je me serai levé.
Tu te fus levé.	Tu te seras levé.
Il se fut levé.	Il se sera levé.
Nous nous fûmes levés.	Nous nous serons levés.
Vous vous fûtes levés.	Vous vous serez levés.
Ils se furent levés.	Ils se seront levés.

CONDITIONAL.

PRESENT.	PAST.
I should rise.	*I should have risen.*
Je me lèverais.	Je me serais levé.
Tu te lèverais.	Tu te serais levé.
Il se lèverait.	Il se serait levé.
Nous nous lèverions.	Nous nous serions levés.
Vous vous lèveriez.	Vous vous seriez levés.

SUBJUNCTIVE.

PRESENT OR FUTURE.
That I may rise.
Que je me lève.
Que tu te lèves.
Qu'il se lève.
Que nous nous levions.
Que vous vous leviez.
Qu'ils se lèvent.

PAST.
That I may have risen.
Que je me sois levé,
Que tu te sois levé,
Qu'il se soit levé, -
Que nous nous soyons levés,
Que vous vous soyez levés,
Qu'ils se soient levés.

IMPERFECT.
That I might rise.
Que je me levasse.
Que tu te levasses.
Qu'il se levât.
Que nous nous levassions.
Que vous vous levassiez.
Qu'il se levassent.

PLUPERFECT.
That I might have risen.
Que je me fusse levé.
Que tu te fusses levé.
Qu'il se fût levé.
Que nous nous fussions levés.
Que vous vous fussiez levés.
Qu'ils se fussent levés.

IMPERATIVE.

Rise (thou).

Lève-toi. Qu'il se lève. Levons-nous. Levez-vous. Qu'ils se lèvent.

125.—CONJUGATION OF A VERB IMPERSONAL.

(See FALLOIR, PLEUVOIR, SEOIR, in the list of irregular verbs, page 72.) Y AVOIR (literally : "there to have") is very frequently used :

INFINITIVE.

PRESENT. — Y avoir,   there to be.
PAST. — Y avoir eu,   there to have been.

PARTICIPLES.

PRESENT. — Y ayant,   there being.
PAST. — Y ayant eu,   there having been.
FUTURE — Devant y avoir, (an idiom meaning, As there is to be).

INDICATIVE.

PRESENT.
There is or *are.*
Il y a.

PAST DEFINITE.
There was or *were.*
Il y eut.

IMPERFECT.
There was or *were.*
Il y avait.

FUTURE.
There will be.
Il y aura.

PAST.
There has or *have been.*
l y a eu.

PAST ANTERIOR.
There had been.
Il y eut eu.

PLUPERFECT.	FUTURE ANTERIOR.
There had been.	*There will have been*
Il y avait eu.	Il y aura eu.

CONDITIONAL.		SUBJUNCTIVE.
PRESENT.	PRESENT OR FUTURE.	IMPERFECT.
There would be.	*That there may be.*	*That there might be.*
Il y aurait.	Qu'il y ait	Qu'il y eût.
PAST.	PAST.	PLUPERFECT.
There would have been.	*That there may have been.*	*That there might have been.*
Il y aurait eu.	Qu'il y ait eu.	Qu'il y eût eu.

127. — GENERAL RULES FOR FORMING THE TENSES.

From the participle present, form:

The three persons plural of the "PRESENT OF THE INDICATIVE" by changing the termination ANT into ONS, EZ, ENT. (Except verbs of Class IV of the second conjugation, and verbs of the third conjugation.)

The "IMPERFECT OF THE INDICATIVE" by changing the ANT into AIS, AIS, AIT, IONS, IEZ, AIENT.

The "PRESENT OF THE SUBJUNCTIVE" by changing the ANT into E, ES, E, IONS, IEZ, and ENT. (Except verbs of Class IV of the second conjugation, and verbs of the third conjugation.)

The "FUTURE OF THE INDICATIVE" and the "CONDITIONAL" are formed from the present of the Infinitive by changing the final R, RE, or OIR, for the future, into RAI, RAS, RA, I ONS, REZ, RONT; (Except verbs of Class IV of the second conjugation.) for the conditional, into RAIS, RAIS, RAIT, RIONS, RIEZ, RAIENT. (Except verbs of Class IV of the second conjugation.)

The "IMPERFECT OF THE SUBJUNCTIVE" is formed from the second person singular of the past definite of the Indicative, by adding another s with E, ES, IONS, IEZ, and ENT; the third person singular ends with T (AT, IT, UT, INT).

The "IMPERATIVE" is like the present of the Indicative, omitting the pronouns. The third persons are like those of the present Subjunctive. When the second person singular of the present of the Indicative ends with ES, s is always suppressed in the Imperative, except in particular cases.

128. — AN ALPHABETICAL LIST OF THE PRINCIPAL IRREGULAR AND DEFECTIVE VERBS.

Throughout the list, wherever the first person is alone given, the other persons are regularly formed according to the synoptical table of terminations.

NOTE. The following is the order in which the tenses are given:— Infinitive present; participle present; participle past; indicative present, imperfect, past definite, future; conditional; imperative; subjunctive present, imperfect.

NOTE. Verbs compounded of a verb and a preposition are conjugated like the verb with which they correspond; thus, COMPRENDRE like PRENDRE, CONSCRIRE like ÉCRIRE (the É of ÉCRIRE is a euphonic letter), etc.

— 71 —

A Verb preceded by an asterisk (*) is defective.

ETRE added to the participle, signifies that the compound tenses are conjugated with that auxiliary; as je suis allé, etc.

*ABSOUDRE, (to absolve.) Absol vant, absou s, fem. absout e—J'absou s —J'absolv ais—J'absoud rai—J'absoud rais—Absou s—Que j'absolv e.

ACQUÉRIR, (to acquire.) Acquér ant, acqui s—J'acquier s, s, t; nous acquér ons, ez, ils acquièr ent—J'acquér ais—J'acqu is—J'acquer rai— J'acquer rais—Acquier s—Que j'acquièr e, es, e, acquér ions, iez, acquièr ent—Que j'acqu isse.

ALLER.(to go.) All ant, all é (être)—Je vais, vas, va; nous all ons, ez, ils vont—J'all ais—J'all ai—J'i rai—J'i rais—Va—Que j'aill e, es, e; allions, iez, aill ent—Que j'all asse.

ASSAILLIR, (to assault.) Assaill ant, assaill i—J'assaill e—J'assaill ais —J'assaill is—J'assailli rai—J'assailli rais—Assaill e—Que j'assaill e— Que j'assaill isse.

ASSEOIR, (s',) (to sit down.) S'assey ant, assis (être)—Je m'assie ds— Je m'assey ais—Je m'ass is—Je m'assi érai—Je m'assi érais—Assie dstoi—Que je m'assey e—Que je m'ass isse.

BATTRE, (to beat.) Batt ant, batt u—Je bat s—Je batt ais—Je battis—Je batt rai—Je batt rais—Bat s—Que je batt e—Que je batt isse.

BOIRE, (to drink.) Buv ant, b u—Je boi s, s, t; buv ons, ez, boiv ent —Je buv ais—Je b us—Je boi rai—Je boi rais—Boi s—Que je boiv e, es, e; buv ions, iez, boiv ent—Que je b usse.

BOUILLIR, (to boil.) Bouill ant, bouill i—Je bou s—Je bouill ais—Je bouill is—Je bouilli rai—Je bouilli rais—Bou s—Que je bouill e—Que je bouill isse.

CONCLURE, (to conclude.) Conclu ant, concl u—Je conclu s—Je conclu ais—Je concl us—Je conclu rai—Je conclu rais—Conclu s—Que je conclu e—Que je concl usse.

CONFIRE, (to pickle.) Confi sant, confi t—Je confi s—Je confi sais— Je confi s—Je confi rai—Je confi rais—Confi s—Que je confi se—Que je conf isse.

COUDRE, (to sew.) Cous ant, cous u—Je coud s—Je cous ais—Je cous is—Je coud rai—Je coud rais—Coud s—Que je cous e—Que je cous isse.

COURIR, (to run.) Cour ant, cour u—Je cour s—Je cour ais—Je cour us—Je cour rai—Je cour rais—Cour s—Que je cour e—Que je cour usse.

CROIRE, (to believe.) Croy ant, cr u—Je croi s—Je croy ais—Je cr us —Je croi rai—Je croi rais—Croi s—Que je croi e—Que je cr usse.

CUEILLIR, (to gather.) Cueill ant, cueill i—Je cueill e—Je cueill ais —Je cueill is—Je cueill erai—Je cueill erais—Cueill e—Que je cuei l Que je cueill isse.

DIRE, (to tell.) Dis ant, di t—Je di s, s, t; dis ons, dites,† dis ent—Je dis ais—Je d is—Je di rai—Je di rais—Di s—Que je dis e—Que je d isse

†DIRE and REDIRE make in the second person plural of the indicative present and of the imperative DITES and REDITES; but the other verbs, compounded of DIRE, follow the general termination—CONTREDISEZ, DÉDISIEZ, INTERDISEZ, MÉDISEZ, PRÉDISEZ.

Écrire, (to write,) Écriv ant, écri t—J'écri s—J'écriv ais—J'écriv is—J'écri rai—J'écri rais—Écri s—Que j'écriv e—Que j'écriv isse.

Envoyer, (to send.) Envoy ant, envoy é—J'envoi e—J'envoy ais—J'envoy ai—J'enver rai—J'enver rais—Envoi e—Que j'envoi e—Que j'envoy asse.

Faire, (to make, to do.) Fais ant, fai t—Je fai s, s, t; fais ons, fait es font—Je fais ais—Je f is—Je fe rai—Je fe rais—Fai s—Que je fass e—Que je f isse.

*Falloir, (to be necessary.) Fall u—Il fau t—Il fall ait—Il fall ut—Il faud ra—Il faud rait—Qu'il faill e—Qu'il fall ût.

Fuir, (to run away.) Fuy ant, fu i—Je fui s—Je fuy ais—Je fu is—Je fui rai—Je fui rais—Fui s—Que je fui e—Que je fu isse.

Hair, (to hate.) Haïss ant, haï—Je hai s, s, t; haïss ons, haïss ez, haïss ent—Je haïss ais—Je haïs—Je haï rai—Je haï rais—Hai s—Que je haïss e—Que je ha ïsse.

Lire, (to read.) Lis ant, l u—Je li s—Je lis ais—Je l us—Je li rai—Je li rais—Li s—Que je lis e—Que je l usse.

*Luire, (to shine.) Luis ant, lu i—Je lui s—Je luis ais—Je lui rai—Je lui rais—Lui s—Que je luis e.

Maudire, (to curse.) Maudiss ant, maudi t—Je maudi s—Je maudiss ais—Je maud is—Je maudi rai—Je maudi rais—Maudi s—Que je maudiss e—Que je maud isse.

† Mettre, (to put.) Mett ant—mi s—Je met s—Je mett ais—Je m is—Je mett rai—Je mett rais—Met s—Que je mett e—Que je m isse.

Moudre, (to grind.) Moul ant—moul u—Je moud s—Je moul ais—Je moul us—Je moud rai—Je moud rais—Moud s—Que je moul e—Que je moul usse.

Mourir, (to die.) Mour ant, mort (être)—Je meur s, s, t; mour ons, ez, meur ent—Je mour ais—Je mour us—Je mour rai—Je mour rais—Meur s—Que je meur e, es, e; mour ions, iez, meur ent—Que je mour usse.

Mouvoir, (to move.) Mouv ant, m u—Je meu s, s, t; mouv ons, ez, meuv ent—Je mouv ais—Je m us—Je mouv rai—Je mouv rais—Meu s—Que je meuv e, es, e; mouvi ons, iez, meuv ent—Que je m usse.

Naitre, (to be born.) Nais sant, n é (être)—Je nai s—Je naiss ais—Je naqu is—Je naît rai—Je naît rais—Nai s—Que je naiss e—Que je naqu isse.

Nuire, (to hurt.) Nuis ant, nu i. The rest like réduire, page 35.

Plaire, (to please.) Plais ant, pl u—Je plai s—Je plais ais—Je pl us—Je plai rai—Je plai rais—Plai s—Que je plais e—Que je pl usse.

Pleuvoir, (to rain.) Pleuv ant, pl u—Il pleu t—Il pleuv ait—Il pl ut—Il pleuv ra—Il pleuv rait—Qu'il pleuv e—Qu'il pl ût.

Pourvoir, (to provide.) Pourvoy ant, pourv u—Je pourvoi s—Je pourvoy ais—Je pourv us—Je pourvoi rai—Je pourvoi rais—Pourvoi s—Que je pourvoi e—Que je pourv usse.

Pouvoir, (to be able.) Pouv ant, p u—Je pui s or je peu x, tu peu x, t; pouv ons, ez, peuv ent—Je pouv ais—Je p us—Je pour rai—Je pour rais—Que je puiss e—Que je p usse.

Prendre, (to take.) Pren ant, pri s—Je pren ds, ds, d; pren ons, ez, prenn ent—Je pren ais—Je pr is—Je prend rai—Je prend rais—Prend s—Que je prenn e, es, e; pren ions, iez, prenn ent—Que je pr isse.

— 73 —

PRÉVALOIR, (to prevail.) Like VALOIR, except subjunctive present, que je préval e, etc.

PRÉVOIR,'(to foresee). Like VOIR, except je prévoi rai, je prévoi rais.

RÉSOUDRE, (to resolve). Résolv ant, résol u and résou s—Je résou s—Je résolv ais—Je résol us—Je résoud rai — Je résoud rais—Résou s—Que je résolv e—Que 'e résol ussè.

RIRE, (to laugh). Ri ant, ri—Je ri s—Je ri ais—Je ri s—Je ri rai— Je ri rais—Ri s—Que je ri e—Que je ri sse.

ROMPRE, (to break. Romp ant, romp u—Je romp s—Je romp ais—Je romp is—Je romp rai—Je romp rais—Romp s—Que je romp e — Que je romp isse.

SAVOIR, (to know). Sach ant, s u—Je sai s, s, t ; sav ons, ez, sav ent—Je sav ais—Je s us—Je sau rai—Je sau rais—Sach e, sach ons, sach ez—Que Je sach e—Que je s usse.

SEOIR, (to be becoming, suit.) Sey ant—Il si ed—Il sey ait — Il sié ra —Il sié rait—Qu'il sié e.

*SEOIR, (to sit). Sé ant, sitting—S is (situated).

SUFFIRE, (to suffice). Suffis ant, suffi. Like CONFIRE.

SUIVRE, (to follow). Suiv ant, suiv i—Je sui s—Je suiv ais—Je suiv is —Je suiv rai—Je suiv rais—Sui s—Que je suiv e—Que je suiv isse.

TAIRE, (to conceal) (SE TAIRE, to be silent). Like PLAIRE.

*TRAIRE, (to milk). Tray ant, trai t—Je trai s—Je tray ais—Je trai rai Je trai rais—Trai s—Que je trai e.

VAINCRE, (to vanquish). Vainqu ant, vainc u—Je vain cs—Je vainqu ais —Je vainqu is—Je vainc rai—Je vainc rais—Vain cs—Que je vainqu e— Que je vainqu isse.

VALOIR, (to be worth). Val ant, val u—Je vau x—Je val ais—Je val us —Je vaud rai—Je vaud rais. No imperative. Que je vaill e, es, e; val ions, iez, vaill ent—Que je val usse.

VETIR, (to clothe). Vêt ant, vêt u—Je vêt s—Je vêt ais—Je vêt is—Je vêti rai—Je vêti rais—Vêt s—Que je vêt e—Que je vêt isse.

VIVRE, (to live). Viv ant, véc u—Je vi s—Je viv ais — Je véc us — Je viv rai—Je viv rais—Vi s—Que je viv e—Que je véc usse.

VOIR, (to see). Voy ant, v u—Je voi s—Je voy ais — Je v is — Je ver-rai—Je ver rais—Voi s—Que je voi e—Que je v isse.

VOULOIR, (to be willing). Je veu x, x, t; voul ons, ez, veul ent—Je voul ais —Je voul us—Je voud rai—Je voud rais—Veuill e, veuill ez—Que je veuill e, es, e; voul ions, iez, veuill ent—Que je voul usse.

AGREEMENT OF THE PARTICIPLE PAST.

129. The past participle after the auxiliary AVOIR (or ETRE in the compound tenses of reflective verbs), is declinable if the objective (accusative) case PRECEDES the participle, and the participle then agrees with the objective (accusative) in gender and number; as,

La lettre que mon frère a écrite.   The letter which my brother has written.

Cette femme s'est proposée pour mo-   That woman has proposed herself as
dèle à ses enfants.   a model to her children.

But if the objective (accusative) is placed after the participle, the participle is indeclinable ; as,

Ma sœur a écrit la lettre.	My sister has written the letter.
Cette femme s'est proposé d'enseigner la géographie à ses enfants.	That woman has intended to teach geography to her children.

The past participle after AVOIR never agrees with its subject (nominative); as,

Ma sœur a parlé.	My sister has spoken.
Elle a écrit.	She has written.

ADVERBS OF QUANTITY

130. Adverbs of quantity, such as AUTANT, ASSEZ, COMBIEN, BEAUCOUP, BIEN, GUÈRE, PEU, QUE, TANT, and TROP, are followed by the preposition DE when used with substantives ; as,

"autant d'amis," as or so many friends.	"Il n'a guère de patience." He has but little patience.
"assez d'argent," money enough.	"peu de connaissances," few acquaintances.
"combien de livres"? how many books ?	"que de travaux !" how many labors!
"beaucoup de richesses," many riches.	"tant de soins," so much care.
"bien des peines," many troubles.	"trop d'occupation," too many occupations.

* See the rule 122.

When used in a general sense, after the above adverbs, the substantives are not preceded by the article ; as, "beaucoup d'argent."

The adverb BIEN is, however, always followed by the article before a substantive; as, "bien de l'argent, bien de la peine," much money, much trouble.

Except when it precedes the word AUTRE, other; as, "bien d'autres disent la même chose," many others say the same thing.

FABLES.

FIRST LESSON.
The fable of the Crow and the Fox.

Un Corbeau s'étant perché sur un arbre pour manger un morceau de fromage qu'il tenait en son bec, un Renard, qui l'aperçut, fut tenté de le lui enlever. Ainsi, pour amuser le Corbeau, il commença à le louer de son plumage. Le Renard, voyant que le Corbeau prenait goût à ses louanges, lui dit : si votre voix est aussi belle que votre corps est beau, vous devez être le plus joli de tous les oiseaux.

Le Corbeau fut si content de ce compliment flatteur, qu'il ouvrit le bec pour montrer qu'il avait la voix belle et laissa tomber le fromage; le fin Renard s'en saisit et le mangea aux yeux du Corbeau, qui demeura tout honteux de sa sottise.

A Crow having perched herself on a tree, in order to eat a piece of cheese which she held in her bill, a Fox that perceived her, was tempted to take it away from her. Therefore, with an intention of alluring the Crow, he began to praise her for the extraordinary beauty of her feathers. The Fox seeing that the Crow took some pleasure in his praises, said to her: if your voice is as fine as your body is beautiful, you must be the most lovely of all birds.

The Crow was so well pleased with this flattering compliment, that she opened her bill in order to show what a fine voice she had, and let fall the piece of cheese; the cunning Fox immediately seized it, and eat it in the crow's sight, who was quite ashamed of her folly.

MORAL.

Les flatteurs sont très dangereux; il faut toujours être en garde contre eux.

Flatterers are very dangerous; we should always be upon our guard against them.

SECOND LESSON.
The fable of the Frog and the Ox.

Une Grenouille ayant un jour aperçu un Bœuf qui paissait dans une prairie, se flatta de pouvoir devenir aussi grosse que cet animal. Elle fit de grands efforts pour enfler sa peau ridée, et demanda alors à ses compagnes si sa taille commençait à approcher de celle du Bœuf.

Elles lui dirent que non. Elle fit donc de nouveaux efforts pour s'enfler toujours de plus en plus, et demanda encore une fois aux Grenouilles si elle égalait à peu près la grosseur du Bœuf.

Elles lui firent la même réponse que la première fois.

La grenouille ne changea pas pour cela de dessein, elle persista; mais le

A Frog spying one day an Ox in a meadow, fancied that she could make herself as big as that animal. She made great efforts to swell the wrinkles of her skin, and asked her companions whether her size began to come near that of the Ox.

They told her that it was not. She therefore made new efforts to swell herself still more and more, and asked a second time of the Frogs, whether she did almost equal the bigness of the Ox.

They made her the same answer as they had before.

The Frog did not, however, change

dernier effort qu'elle fit pour s'enfler fut si violent, qu'elle en creva sur le champ.	her design; but the last effort which she made to swell herself was so violent, that she burst immediately.

MORAL.

Les petits se ruinent souvent, quand ils veulent aller de pair avec les Grands et les imiter.	Little folks ruin themselves, when they attempt to be upon an equality with the Great.

THIRD LESSON.
The Fable of the Fox and the Wolf.

Un Renard étant tombé par hasard dans un puits, était sur le point de se noyer, lorsqu'il aperçut un Loup sur le bord du puits. Il le pria instamment de l'assister dans le péril extrême où il se trouvait, et de lui jeter une corde pour qu'il en pût sortir.	A Fox having fallen by chance into a well, was on the point of being drowned, when he perceived a Wolf on the brink of the well. He earnestly begged of him to assist him in this extreme danger, and to throw him a rope that he might get out of it.
Le Loup, plaignant sa disgrace, lui fit plusieurs questions pour savoir comment il était tombé dans le puits.	The Wolf pitying his misfortune asked him several questions, in order to be informed how he had happened to fall into the well.
Ce n'est pas maintenant le temps de me questionner, ni de discourir, répliqua le Renard; quand vous m'aurez tiré d'ici, je vous expliquerai à loisir toutes les circonstances de cette aventure.	It is not now a time to question me, nor to hold a discourse, replied the fox; when you have drawn me out of the place, I will explain to you, at leisure, all the circumstances of this accident.

MORAL.

Il ne convient pas de haranguer nos amis ni de leur faire des réprimandes quand ils sont en danger. Il faut d'abord les secourir, et ensuite leur parler si l'on a quelque chose à leur dire.	It is not fit to make long speeches to our friends, nor to reprimand them, when they are in any danger. We must immediately assist them, and then speak if we have something to say to them.

FOURTH LESSON.
The Fable of the Wild Boar and the Ass.

Un Ane ayant, par accident, rencontré un sanglier, eut l'impudence de se moquer de lui et de l'insulter.	An Ass having accidentally met with a Wild Board, had the impudence to deride and insult him.
Le Sanglier, frémissant de courroux et grinçant les dents, eut d'abord grande envie de le mettre en pièces, mais, faisant aussitôt réflexion qu'un tel animal n'était pas digne de sa colère et de sa vengeance, il se retint.	The Wild Boar, foaming with rage and grinding his teeth, had, at first, a great mind to tear him in pieces; but immediately reflecting that such an animal was not worthy his anger and revenge, he refrained from doing him any harm.
Misérable que tu es, lui dit-il, je te punirais sévèrement si tu en valais la peine, mais je ne veux pas me souiller du sang d'une aussi vile bête. Tu	Poor wretch, said he to him, I could severely punish thee for thy audaciousness if thou wert worthy my notice; but I will not stain myself

n'es qu'un Ane, et ta lâcheté te met à couvert de mes coups et te sauve la vie. Après lui avoir fait ces reproches, il le laissa aller.

with the blood of so mean a beast. Thou art but an Ass, and thy cowardice secures thee against my revenge. After having upbraided him so, he let him go away.

MORAL.

Le mépris est l'unique vengeance que l'on doive prendre d'un sot, ou d'un malheureux. D'ailleurs, la victoire que l'on remporte sur un vil et faible ennemi est trop aisée et ne fait pas bonneur.

Contempt is the only revenge which we ought to take of a silly fellow, or of an impudent wretch. Besides, the victory which is gained over a weak and paltry enemy, is too easy and does not procure honor.

FIFTH LESSON.

The Fable of the Lion and the Rat.

Un Lion, fatigué de la chaleur et abattu de lassitude, dormait à l'ombre d'un arbre. Un Rat, qui le vit, lui monta sur le corps pour se divertir. Le Lion se réveilla, étendit la patte, et s'en saisit; le Rat, se voyant ainsi pris et sans espérance d'échapper, demanda pardon au Lion de son incivilité et de sa hardiesse et le supplia très humblement de lui sauver la vie. Le Lion, touché de cette soumission, le laissa aller.

Ce bienfait ne fut pas perdu; car, le Lion étant tombé, quelques jours après, dans un filet dont il ne pouvait se débarrasser, il se mit à rugir de toute sa force. Le Rat, reconnaissant aux rugissements du Lion qu'il était pris, accourut promptement pour le secourir; il se mit aussitôt à ronger les mailles du filet, et lui procura par là un moyen de s'évader.

A Lion faint with heat and weary with fatigue slept under a shady tree. A Rat, that saw him, got upon his back, to have a little sport. The Lion, waking, stretched his paw, and took him; the Rat finding himself taken, and without hopes of escaping, asked the Lion's pardon for his boldness, and very humbly craved for his life. The Lion, moved by his submission, let him go.

This favor was not lost; for the Lion, being caught a few days after in a net, from which he could not free himself, he began to roar mightily. The Rat knowing by the Lion's roaring that he was taken, ran quickly to his assistance; he began instantly to gnaw the meshes of his net, and thereby enabled him to make his escape.

MORAL.

En excusant une petite faute, on se procure souvent l'affection de celui à qui l'on a pardonné.

By forgiving a small fault we often secure the affection of the trangressor.

SIXTH LESSON.

The Fable of the Bird-catcher and the Stork.

Ce pauvre oiseau le pria avec instance de lui sauver la vie et de lui rendre la liberté; d'autant qu'elle n'était ni Oie, ni Grue, et qu'elle ne faisait de tort à personne.

De plus, dit-elle, j'ai grand soin de ma vieille mère et la nourris avec toute l'attention dont je suis capable.

L'oiseleur impitoyable lui répondit avec aigreur: qu'est-ce que cela m'importe ? puisque te voilà prise avec les autres qui m'ont fait du tort, tu mourras avec eux.

This unfortunate Bird entreated him earnestly to spare her life, and to set her at liberty, as she was neither a Goose nor a Crane, and did no harm to any body.

Besides, said she, I take great care of my old mother, and feed her with all the attention I am capable of.

The unmerciful bird-catcher answered her, with an angry tone, what is all that to me ? since thou art now taken with others that have done me harm, thou shalt also die with them.

MORAL.

Il ne faut jamais fréquenter que des gens de bien; car ceux qui s'associent avec les méchants, périront avec eux, quoiqu'ils soient innocents.

We must never associate with any other but good people; for those who keep company with the wicked will suffer with them, though they may be innocent.

SEVENTH LESSON.

The Fable of the Horse and the Fly.

Une Mouche, placée sur le timon d'une voiture, criait d'un ton impérieux après le Cheval qui la tirait : que tu vas lentement ! ne veux-tu pas marcher plus vite ? Prends garde que je te perce le cou de mon aiguillon.

Le Cheval lui répondit froidement: tes paroles et tes menaces ne me touchent guère; je ne crains que celui qui conduit, avec un fouet long et souple, le joug que je porte; c'est pourquoi cesse de me parler avec cet air frivole et téméraire.

Car je sais mieux que toi quand il faut m'arrêter, et quand je dois courir.

A Fly sitting upon the pole of a carriage, called to the Horse that was drawing it : how slowly you creep along ! won't you mend your pace and go faster ? Take care or I shall twinge your neck with the weapon I have.

The Horse, with an air of contempt, replied: your commands and threats are not worth my notice; I only dread the man, who whith his long and pliant whip drives the burden which I bear; therefore leave off speaking to me in that saucy and impertinent manner.

For I know better than you can tell me, when to halt, and when to mend my pace.

MORAL.

Cette fable sert à exposer l'impudente hardiesse et le ridicule déportement de ces gens, qui, sans avoir ni force ni pouvoir, ne laissent pas pourtant de faire de vaines menaces.

This fable serves to expose the impudent boldness and ridiculous behaviour of those people, who, having neither abilities nor power, dare, nevertheless, utter vain and disdainful

RECUEIL DE BONS MOTS.

A physician, who lived in London, visited a lady who lived at Chelsea: after he had continued his visits for some time, the lady expressed an apprehension, that it might be inconvenient to him to come so far on her account. Oh madam, replied the doctor, I have another patient in this neighbourhood, and by that means, you know, "I kill two birds with one stone."

A lady's age happening to be questioned, she affirmed it was but forty, and called upon a gentleman, who was in the company, to deliver his opinion. Cousin, said she, do you believe I am right, when I say I am but forty? "I'm sure, madam," said he, "I ought not to dispute it; for I have constantly heard you say so for above these ten years."

An Irishman, being asked if he understood French, replied: "Yes, joy, I understand French perfectly well, provided it's spoken in Irish."

A gentleman having lent a guinea for two or three days to a person whose promises he had not much faith in, was very much surprised to find that he very punctually kept his word with him. The same gentleman being some time after desirous of borrowing a large sum, "No," said the other, "you have deceived me once, and I am resolved you shall not do it a second time."

An English gentleman asked sir R. Steele, who was an Irishman, what was the reason that his countrymen were so remarkable for blundering, and making bulls? "Faith," said the knight, "I believe there is something in the air of Ireland; and I dare say, if an Englishman were born there, he would do the same."

A man, complaining to a friend that his wife's drunkenness and ill conduct had almost ruined him, concluded, as the vulgar usually do, and "for goodness' sake, what's to be said for it? Nothing that I know," said his friend, "can be said, *for* it, but much *against* it."

An Irishman having a looking-glass in his hand, shut his eyes, and placed it before his face: another asking him why he did so, "Upon my shoul," says Teague, "it ish to shee how I look when I am ashleep."

Lord Chesterfield was asked at court one day, what he thought of lady Coventry, whose complexion was evidently of her own manufacture: "Really," replied his lordship, "I am no connaisseur in painting."

An Italian gentleman, who was dangerously ill, and at the same time heavily charged with debts, told his confessor, that the only favour he had to ask of heaven was that his life might be prolonged till he had discharged them. Then, replied the priest, since your reason for wishing to live is so just, I pray that your prayers may be heard. Ay! father, answered the sick man, I pray that they may; "for I am sure, if I live till I pay my debts, I shall never die."

Some robbers having broke into a gentleman's house, they went to the footman's bed, and told him, if he moved he was a dead man. "That's a d—d lie," cried the fellow; "if I move, I am sure I am alive."

Lord Mansfield, being willing to save a man who had stolen a gewgaw trinket, desired the jury to value it at *ten pence*; upon which the prosecutor cries out: "Ten pence," my lord! why the very "fashion" of it cost me ten times the sum. Oh! says his lordship, we must not hang a man for "fashion's sake."

If you marry, said a father to his daughter, you will do well; if you do not marry, you will do better. If that's the case, replied the daughter, get me a husband as soon as you can: I shall be content to do *well*; I leave it to others to do *better*.

A certain country squire ask'd a "Merry Andrew" why he played the fool. "For the same reason," said he, "that you do, out of *want*: you do it for *want* of wit, I do it for *want* of money.

A countryman was sowing a field, and two smart fellows happening to ride that way, one of them called to him with an insolent air: Well, honest fellow, 'tis your business to sow; but we reap the fruits of your labour. To which the countryman replied: "Tis very likely you may, truly; for I am sowing hemp."

A gentleman, who had the character of a great punster, was desired one night in company, by a gentleman, to make a "pun extempore." Upon what subject? said Daniel. The *king*, answered the other. "Oh! sir," said he, "the king is no subject."

A Scotchman was very angry with an English gentleman, who, he said, had abused him, and called him "false Scot." "Indeed" said the Englishman, "I said no such thing; I said you were a *true* Scot.

In a visit queen Elizabeth made to the famous lord chancellor Bacon, at a small country-seat, which he had built for himself before his preferment, she asked him how it came that he made himself so small a house. "It is not I, madam," answered he, "who have made my house too small for myself, but your Majesty who has made me too big for my house.'

END.

www.ingramcontent.com/pod-product-compliance
Lightning Source LLC
Chambersburg PA
CBHW020330090426
42735CB00009B/1475